THE OUTLAWS

Tales of Bad Guys
Who Shaped the Wild West

ROBERT BARR SMITH

TWODOT®

GUILFORD, CONNECTICUT
HELENA, MONTANA
AN IMPRINT OF GLOBE PEQUOT PRESS

To buy books in quantity for corporate use
or incentives, call **(800) 962–0973**
or e-mail **premiums@GlobePequot.com.**

A · T W O D O T® · B O O K

TwoDot is an imprint of Globe Pequot Press and a registered trademark of Morris Book Publishing, LLC.

Project Editor: Tracee Williams
Layout: Casey Shain

Library of Congress Cataloging-in-Publication Data

Smith, Robert B. (Robert Barr), 1933-
The outlaws : tales of bad guys who shaped the Wild West / Robert Barr Smith.
pages cm
Includes bibliographical references and index.
ISBN 978-0-7627-9135-4
1. Outlaws—West (U.S.)—History—Anecdotes. 2. West (U.S.)—History—1890-1945—Anecdotes. 3. West (U.S.)—History—1860-1890—Anecdotes. 4. Frontier and pioneer life—West (U.S.)—Anecdotes. I. Title.
F595.S66 2013
978'.02—dc23

2013015028

Printed in the United States of America

10 9 8 7 6 5 4 3 2 1

CONTENTS

INTRODUCTION

YOU DON'T HAVE TO learn about the Old West from the silver screen, which usually gets it all wrong. The best way to find out what frontier America was really like is to read her newspapers. Sometimes pompous, often flowery, they still reflect what life—and death—were like way out west.

The people who pushed west were mostly ordinary folks, the guts of the young United States, tough, ambitious, hardworking, and anxious to leave the world better for their kids than it had been for them. Those who did not come of that hardy stock did not last.

They were mostly farmers, eager to come to grips with the new land. And the professional people who made the same arduous trip—the doctors and lawyers and clergymen and teachers—were the same kind of men and women, ready to take on this new country and tame it.

And with them came the troublemakers, to everybody's sorrow. Some of them were already running from the law someplace else. Others were simply dishonest, looking for a time and place to blossom into full-blown hoodlums. Some of the young people emulated them: There was some illusory swagger in being a hoodlum; witness the nicknames they carried around, many of which they had invented themselves, a sort of phony glory.

For example, one of the Dalton Boys' early associates was a hoodlum whose mother had named him plain Bill McElhanie, but Bill preferred to call himself the Narrow-Gauge Kid. Like this "kid," a good many western outlaws acquired nicknames during their mostly brief careers, some of them pretty outlandish.

There were Bittercreek and Black-Faced Charlie; Dynamite Jack and Dynamite Dick; Pegleg and Cockeye Charlie and Little Dick; Curly Bill, Wild Bill, Cherokee Bill, Old Bill, and Polka-Dot Bill; Texas Billy and Wyoming Frank; Red Buck and Tulsa Jack.

Not to mention Broken Nose and Flat Nose; Turkey Creek and Buckskin Frank; Black Jack (a couple of those) and Three-Fingered

Jack; Billy the Kid and Harry the Kid; the Sundance Kid and the Mormon Kid; the Narrow-Gauge Kid and the Verdigris Kid.

And so on.

Some of the criminal element were psychotic, some simply immoral; others just chose to be criminals because it beat working all hollow, or it seemed to. The newspapers caught the spirit of the moment, and the grief and pathos of it. Take this newspaper account of a frontier social event:

> At a dance . . . one night last week one Royal Junking let off
> his Winchester in the midst of a row. The ball wounded two
> men in the arm, passed through the wall, killed a dog on the
> outside and entered a tree. The dance then proceeded.

Nothing was to be allowed to interfere with such small pleasures as there were. But sometimes there was no element of humor, simply anger and injury and death—for example, this story in the *Muskogee Phoenix* of July 1896:

> A serious shooting affray is reported from Oolagah. Eli
> Rogers shot and instantly killed Nick Rogers and at the same
> time Sharp Rogers shot and instantly killed Nick Rogers and
> at the same time Sharp Rogers was shot by Sam Rogers. The
> trouble began at Huse Rogers' house . . . and is the result
> of an old feud. . . . The killing is the outcome of the fight
> in which Bub Trainor lost his life more than a year ago. The
> shot received by Sharp Rogers will prove fatal.

This was Indian Territory, but the same sorts of ugly things happened elsewhere across the West. A nation was being born, a mighty nation, but the labor pains were sometimes terrible.

This book is about the men—and a few women—who made a career of stealing things other people had worked for . . . and killing anybody who objected. There was nothing of Robin Hood about these criminals; they were the trash of the West and should be remembered as that and nothing more.

Chapter 1

BAD MEN

ROBBERS ARE WITH US TODAY and always will be, like taxes and the flu. They come in all kinds: gangs, individuals, grandmothers, hard-up gamblers, terrorists, people in Darth Vader masks, idiots with cap pistols. There are the yellow punks who rob convenience stores, preferably those with only a single female clerk, and the teenage jackals who mob a store and swiftly carry off whatever takes their fancy. These are the same hoodlums who roll elderly ladies for their Social Security checks and steal from the church poor box.

They all make the news, but only briefly, and they are mostly pale imitations of those who made unauthorized withdrawals back in the days of the horseback bandit and in the first three decades of the last century. Back then they robbed anything that moved: trains and stagecoaches and individuals, plus banks and country stores and little farmsteads.

Particularly in the 1920s and '30s, when bank robbery was really in flower, the newspapers tended to glamorize the thugs who made a business of robbing folks; it sold papers, after all, and that was the important thing. And newspapers were far more important in those far-off times, since television, mercifully, was only a dream. Sadly, some writers then—like some today—were somewhat less than scrupulous when it came to reporting facts: If the truth was not quite exciting enough, what did it matter if it grew some in the telling? As long as it sold papers, that is.

For example, some enterprising journalistic hack published the exciting, not to say astounding, tale of a robbery perpetrated by three of the most notorious scoundrels of the '30s, Pretty Boy Floyd and a couple of other hoodlums of similar notoriety. The trouble with that was that one of the trio was in jail at the time and one was out of the country. Where the third was is not clear. So much for journalistic integrity, or maybe it was only a disdain for accuracy in that case.

And then the movies took over, usually romanticizing these hoodlums a bit or a bunch, telling their story without any apparent regard to what they were like or what they actually did. Then came television, which not only created its own notion of the old-time robbers but continued to show the movies cranked out about them over the years.

Hence the enduring legend of the American robber, by our own day sanitized a bit but still fascinating. As the bandits fade further and further into the misty past, they become less and less flesh and blood and more and more sorts of icons, almost heroic symbols of another day. But they were real enough, and this book tries to paint them as they really were: vicious, depraved, and worthless.

Then there was David Rudabaugh, commonly known as Dirty Dave. He was so called not just for his vile criminal behavior, which was bad enough. He was also famous—or infamous—for his penetrating odor, which was said to precede him by a quarter of an hour. He was, as the Las Vegas New Mexico *Optic* succinctly put it,

> an "all around desperado" . . . equally proficient
> in holding up a railroad train or a stage coach or,
> as occasion offered, robbing a bank, 'shooting up'
> a frontier settlement, or running off stock.

And that was on his good days.

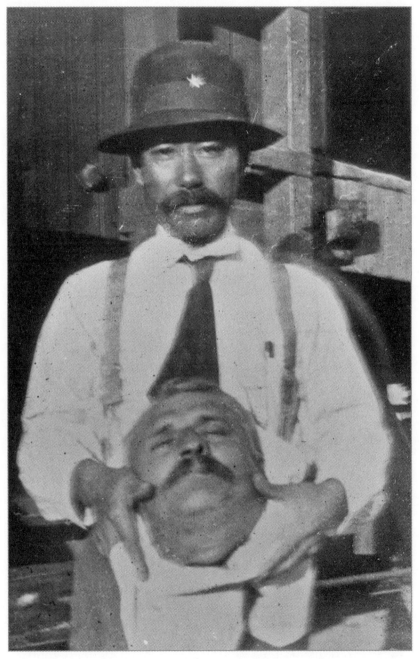

Dirty Dave Rudabaugh's head.

Dirty Dave was also a murderer, who ran with Billy the Kid, Hoodoo Brown's gaggle of crooks in Las Vegas, and finally with the Cowboy Faction down in Tombstone country.

Finally Dave took shelter from the law down in Chihuahua, where he played bully in the hamlet of Parral . . . until the day he got upset during a poker game and killed a couple of the players in a *cantina*. The place emptied forthwith, but later, when Dave returned to the *cantina* after a vain search for his horse, he found a number of citizens waiting.

Dave did not survive the meeting and, as a tasteful additional touch, the locals removed his head. It was then impaled on a pole, complete with hat and scruffy mustache, and paraded around town as the centerpiece of a sort of *ad hoc* fiesta.

It is not recorded that anybody mourned.

Some outlaws had class of a sort, a certain panache, the stuff of maidens' dreams, Robin Hood reincarnate, at least the way the newspapers put it. One of these was Choc Floyd, called Pretty Boy, who liked to joke good-naturedly with bank personnel and frightened customers while filling a sack with their money.

And Choc was a good ol' boy, open-handed with the folks back home in the Cookson Hills of eastern Oklahoma and western Arkansas . . . at least he was until the law finally caught up with him and left him very dead in an Iowa farmer's field. That sort of widespread largesse sure helped your image, especially if you were on the run, and a good many robbers did it. In Choc's case he was basically just a country boy who genuinely liked to see his neighbors happy.

But even when they had not been direct beneficiaries of outlaw handouts, the fact that the robbers gave away money made hard-up country people reluctant to say anything to the law. There was also some danger attached to talking to the authorities. And nobody liked banks much—particularly in hard times, depression times, when foreclosures destroyed and scattered families and hurt business with the local tradesmen.

When the FBI came along, it helped the papers build the illusory image of the romantic criminal. The list of "public enemies"

Four men lynched.

the Bureau created tended to draw them a little larger than life, certainly larger than they were.

One outlaw drawn much bigger than life was John Dillinger, who was considered an aristocrat of the trade, several cuts above ordinary robbers. It was he who famously sneered that Bonnie Parker and Clyde Barrow "gave bank robbery a bad name." And Dillinger did have a certain amount of class, at least by comparison with murderous thugs like Wilber Underhill, who appears later in this book.

Dillinger took a lot of other people's hard-earned money and became famous after a fashion. But in the end he made the mistake of squiring Anna Sage to Chicago's Biograph Theater and met the law on the way out; he ended up dead in the gunfight that followed, but at least he got to see the show and the theater was air-conditioned.

John Dillinger added to the Robin Hood myth, and of course Anna Sage became the Lady in Red. Anybody who survived in the robbery business for more than a couple of months tended to acquire either a halo or horns, or at least an aura of some kind, the journalism of the times being what it was. They all were what the headlines made them. The journalists often overlooked the fact that these same people were a clear and present danger to everybody, not just bankers and police officers.

There has been so much good stuff written about Dillinger that he appears only as a shadow in this book—you can see the bibliography for further reading. But I cannot resist one Dillinger tale. It ranks right up there with the wonderful fable of a lawman told with a straight face by a history writer. According to myth, this

> deadly lawman carried his revolver in front of his belt instead of behind, so that by a quick muscular movement of the stomach he can toss the pistol into his hand before his adversary has time to draw on him.

Why, sure he could. Maybe he could throw a grenade that way, too.

There are any number of Dillinger anecdotes, but my favorite is the tale of the great escape, with Dillinger armed—in popular tradition—with a fake pistol whittled out of a piece of wood. It made great copy, but sadly it wasn't quite accurate. What he brandished was not a real gun, surely, but a carefully made imitation.

If you kept your hand covering the rudimentary butt, this model would fool almost anybody—and did. It was probably smuggled in to Dillinger—he sure didn't whittle it—but he made the most of it, helped in his play-acting by his formidable reputation. In fact, the "pistol" had a metal barrel made from a razor handle and had a couple of headless nails as sights. But it worked; it fooled his jailers long enough for him to acquire two Thompsons, and then he was on his way.

The all-time high scorer among bank robbers—in terms of number of banks, although certainly not in money made—was probably Henry Starr. Or at least he said so. Starr said a lot of things, most of them false and self-serving, but he may even have been right about his robbing record. Henry along with Belle Starr is one of the greatest characters in mythology since Aesop's fables.

Henry started out when bank robbers fled on horseback and finished his career in the automobile age. "I robbed more banks than any other man," he said while he was dying of a bank man's bullet. Maybe so, maybe not.

It was his second serious wound at the hands of a civilian, and his last. He professed a late belief that crime did not pay, but then he was on the verge of meeting the Ultimate Judge, and that may have concerned even Starr, who was never famous for lofty ethical standards. He certainly had the dubious distinction of writing the ultimate

Henry Starr's mug shot.

AUTHOR'S COLLECTION

outlaw apologia, a very bad, very whiny book called *Thrilling Events*, in which he blamed everybody but himself for his woes.

All in all, though, people who glory in the "romance" of a life of crime ought to remember that the flight, combat, and sudden riches of Starr's line of work got him shot during two different holdups, and won him a couple of jail terms into the bargain—and ultimately got him killed. Not much of a payoff for years of work.

He certainly saw it all. The trouble was, a good deal of it he saw between prison bars or from a hospital bed.

And then there was the man who *really* has a claim to be king of the bank robbers. His name was Harvey Bailey, and he was a far more efficient bandit indeed. He was a whiz until the law caught up with him. But at least he didn't end up dead. He appears in the chapter called "Pro."

Bonnie Parker and Clyde Barrow won a certain renown, in part, probably, because gun-toting girl robbers weren't all that common. And the pair were heavily armed with automatic weapons and quick to use them, and drove madly about the countryside in the salad days of the automobile. They share a chapter later on, although they'd doubtless be disappointed in it: Nothing much flattering is said about them; they left too many widows and orphans in their wake for that.

And then there were the real pros, men like Harvey Bailey, Pretty Boy Floyd, Machinegun Kelly, Machinegun Jack McGurn, Frank "Jelly" Nash, Alvin Karpis—known to many as Creepy Karpis—Adam Richetti, and a host of other famous names. They too became icons of a sort, but the quality of robbers went sharply downhill from there.

The Cookson Hills of eastern Oklahoma were a veritable breeding ground for small-time robbers and killers in the '20s and '30s. Many of that special breed of scum are almost forgotten now, but in their day—usually short—they were a major problem to honest folk.

The Hills spawned a whole regiment of these hoodlums, maybe a combination of Depression-era hard times with the "romance" of the robbery profession. The Cookson boys probably ought to be remembered in a little more detail than you can engrave on a tombstone, so they get a little space in this book.

The renaissance of crime during the '20s and '30s was especially aggravating because these Depression days came before the advent of the FDIC in 1934, and a little bank that had no private deposit insurance might well go belly-up if a robbery cleaned it out. Just as bad, if a bank were robbed often enough, even its private insurance might be canceled, a disaster that did hit several banks. Financial ruin was the result for a lot of small-town folks, mom-and-pop merchants, teachers and doctors and small farmers.

The Depression days meant not only a sharp increase in the incidence of bank robberies but also a simultaneous rise in law enforcement capability, not least in transportation. When Henry Starr, called the Bearcat, started in taking other people's money, he galloped out of town in the good old-fashioned way, on horseback. But by the time he finished his earthly race, the internal combustion engine had arrived. It didn't do Starr any good, but generally speaking it gave the Depression-era robber unprecedented mobility.

Now the law had to try to catch the bank robber who could vanish at high speed after a job—and cars traveling on pavement don't leave tracks.

And hard-surface motor roads offered even more opportunity for the inventive criminal. Take, for example, Pistol Hill in Osage County, Oklahoma. This very steep stretch of road—between the towns of Whizbang (it had a real name, but nobody used it) and Shidler—was a choice spot for criminals. Drivers had to slow down so much that they were sitting ducks for holdups by criminals jumping out on both sides of the road.

The story goes that outlaws stopped and robbed at least one drill-rig crew—some gang members, at least, ended up decorating the walking beam of a well. The local law was said to be unconcerned, the county having been saved a considerable amount of money for trials and such. A nice tale; you hope it's true.

Armament had improved as well as transportation. The Thompson submachine gun had appeared on the scene, and in those days any civilian could buy one. They not only provided the bank robber with an enormous chunk of firepower, but also had a tremendous intimidation effect, even more than the old standby, the large-bore shotgun, which remained the other weapon of choice.

With the advent of the Thompson and the advance in motor power, the bandits should have gained a substantial advantage. It remained to be seen whether law enforcement would keep pace; The police and FBI speedily erased any doubt about that, acquiring their own Thompsons and adding the occasional Browning Automatic Rifle, then the army's standard squad automatic weapon. Grenades made their appearance as well, useful for forted-up hoodlums who wouldn't surrender.

But of course the law was, as always, spread thin. Since the outlaws always had the advantage of surprise, and could carefully recon their target and their escape route, it would seem a wonder that anybody ever got caught. But they did, in large numbers. The reasons for their short careers were several.

First and foremost, and in large part, there was stupidity. Very few of the criminal fraternity were very bright to start with, and many were terminally dense. They often overlooked the most basic details, or shot off their mouths before or after a job—or both—about what big tough outlaws they were. They did astonishing things such as letting their masks fall off, sticking up towns where people knew them well, failing to top up their gas tanks in preparation for flight, and similar moronic mistakes.

Take Wesley Rush, nicknamed Shine in honor of his fondness for bootleg rotgut. He came out of the Oklahoma oil patch, part of a large, more or less lawless family. At least, several of Shine's brothers were bootleggers. And the Rush family had to survive the murder of several of those brothers, one of whom had been fooling around with a thirteen-year-old girl. The man who shot him may have mistaken him for Shine. Another brother was killed by an officer—bank robbery, what else?—and still another was killed in a dance hall fight.

It was almost inevitable that with such a cultivated background, Shine began to run with the big dogs of the criminal world. One was Adam Richetti, a reputed follower of Pretty Boy Floyd himself. Richetti had started out small, running unsuccessfully with some nickel-and-dime crooks, but he advanced in his chosen work until he reached the very top: the electric chair.

Shine did not progress much as a career criminal, although at one time it was thought that he might have followed Floyd himself. But with Shine it was the same old thing: small banks, country stores. Various of Shine's dead-end associates were caught or blown away by the law, but for a while he managed to stay one jump ahead of the forces of law and order.

Along the way the police got some shot into him as he tried to escape arrest. Finally, in 1934, Rush was run down, probably on a tip; the big, bad outlaw was sound asleep in his farmhouse hideout, and there was no resistance.

That was the start of a long stay as a guest of the government, during which Rush became something few other criminals ever managed. If he didn't exactly reform, he at least decided the risk of robbing people wasn't worth the meager rewards. On one occasion he was even invited to join a mass jailbreak, but he declined, reputedly saying that he had had enough of that sort of thing. He did his time and returned to the anonymity from which he came. At least he learned something.

Most of the rest of them did not.

Chapter 2

ROBBERS ON HORSEBACK

AS EVERY KID KNOWS, or thinks he does, the Old West was full of elusive outlaws, famous names like Billy the Kid, the Daltons, the Youngers, Frank and Jesse James, and the like, repeatedly featured in the endless western films we kids got to see at the Saturday matinee.

People called these films horse operas, and they were cheap—fifteen cents when I started to go—and often both ends of a double feature were westerns, along with an installment or two of Rocketman or Buck Rogers, Bugs Bunny pursued by Elmer Fudd, the newsreel, the previews, and ads for the local Chevy dealer and the corner grocery. Popcorn was a nickel. You could wallow in film half a day for a quarter.

That those films were wildly inaccurate never occurred to us kids, and we thought we learned about the Old West from their contrived plots, however unlikely they were in fact. In the old black-and-white movie days, Hollywood ground out Jesse James, Billy the Kid, and Dalton Gang movies thirteen to the dozen.

I remember one that starred Henry Fonda as Frank James and, I think, Tyrone Power as Jesse. The thesis was that the brothers were driven to the outlaw life when the brutal railroad drove their mother out of the old homestead—a thing, of course, that never happened. There were a couple dozen such movies, none of them accurate, some of them very bad indeed.

Two dead Daltons, Bob (left) and Grat (right),
unidentified lawman (live) in the middle.

Jesse even made it to Germany, in a comic strip in which the major player, called Lucky Luke, rode his genius horse Jolly Jumper around dealing with a series of outlaws. The Daltons were a part of the action; they came in four sizes, and all of them looked a lot like Adolf Hitler. Luke and Jolly Jumper dealt with the James boys, too. It was corny, but at that a lot better than some of the American western outlaw movies.

The absolute worst film about the James-Younger Gang was a well-cast, well-acted film called *The Great Northfield Minnesota Raid*. In fact, the citizens of that little town stood up gallantly to the most notorious gang in American history and routed them. The film, however, portrayed the townspeople as venal and cowardly, and in addition to much other nonsense invented a bank embezzlement that never happened.

The James brothers were alumni of Missouri Bushwhacker gangs, and so was Cole Younger. While most Civil War fighters settled down peaceably after the shooting stopped, the James boys and Youngers just carried on. They did not settle down, or try to, but robbed and murdered for eleven years after Appomattox.

They had a long run, and they were mostly successful, often "hoorahing" towns, riding up and down the street yelling and shooting, driving the population indoors while they robbed whatever it was, generally a bank. But with largely unalloyed success sometimes comes arrogance, and that ailment infected the James-Younger Gang.

They decided to try the bank-robbing trade up in Minnesota, where they had never been. It was unknown country to them, and they traveled north apparently in reliance on the rosy picture painted by an outlaw who had.

If their reconnaissance was ineffectual, their execution of the robbery was even worse. In the first place, they seemed not to understand that Northfield was a peaceful place where most people traveled by wagon or buggy and nobody carried a gun. And so, riding fine saddle horses and clanking with weaponry, they naturally attracted some attention.

They probably thought the little town would be an easy mark, which only made their inept attack even less effective. Three of them rode into town, dismounted near the bank, and sat down on some boxes, trying to look like harmless loafers. Two more dismounted in front of the bank, where Cole Younger pretended to tighten his saddle girth. Three more waited just across the river to gallop in and cow the town. As it turned out, Northfield didn't cow worth a hoot.

The gang just didn't fit in—quiet little Northfield was a civilized town where nobody carried a gun or wore a long duster like the gang members did. The gang wore their dusters—they could have taken them off—and were obviously heavily armed. "Those men will bear watching," said one citizen.

Said another, Sim Allen, a hardware store owner, "I don't like the look of them. I believe they are here to rob the bank." Allen was so worried that he tried to enter the bank when the outlaws did.

And then one of the gang members—Clel Miller—made the ultimate colossal mistake. There on a busy street full of people, he pulled a pistol and shoved it in Allen's face; he ordered Allen "not to holler" and said he'd blow Allen's head off if he did. The fat was in the fire. Allen ran yelling down the street and citizens converged to defend their town.

Dense Clel Miller made things worse by firing a shot after Allen. If anybody in town was in doubt that there was trouble down at the bank, they weren't any longer.

The outlaws murdered two unarmed, inoffensive men, one of whom was the bank's cashier. He gallantly refused to open the safe, staunchly pretending that it was on a time lock. He was apparently shot down because they didn't believe him; they were right, the safe was open, but none of the outlaws bothered to try the handle. They couldn't find the cash drawer either.

Nobody knows who murdered the cashier. It was probably Frank James, although one account credits Jesse, inventing some juicy dialog to decorate the notion, thus:

Open it, said Jesse, or you die like a dog.
I will do my duty, said the cashier.

Then die, said Jesse.

Jesse never repeated his word the second time.

The cashier fell, dead.

In the end two of the gang—Miller was one—never rode out of Northfield again. Of the others, at least three were wounded, maybe more, and they galloped out of town, running for their lives. And to add insult to injury, the take was some twenty-six dollars.

People were blazing away at the gang from all directions, bells were ringing and dogs barking all over town, and three gallant citizens stood on a corner throwing rocks at the gang, "big and formidable missiles, more fit for the hand of Goliath than for the sling of David," the newspaper poetically wrote.

The gang's only chance at freedom and safety was to quickly leave Minnesota far behind them, but it soon appeared that they had done no recon of an escape route.

So those cocky, experienced, big-time outlaws got lost and wandered through pouring rain while as many as a thousand men searched for them. And at last they committed the ultimate stupidity: They abandoned their horses, apparently on the peculiar theory that nobody would pay attention to men on foot . . . no rocket scientists, these.

Having given away their last chance at survival, abandoned by the James brothers, the remaining four were found by a posse from Madelia, a town not far from Northfield. In a close-range shoot-out, the citizens killed one of them and captured the three Youngers, all painfully wounded. They would spend many years in prison—and at that they were lucky: Since they had wantonly murdered the two unarmed men in Northfield, only their pleas of guilty saved them from the gallows.

But there was a bright side. Like Elmer McCurdy, whom we'll meet later, the three dead outlaws embarked on a second career, this one useful to society and requiring no special training or education. They became cadavers on which future doctors could practice and learn. It was surely the most public-spirited thing they had ever done.

Even the experienced criminal is not immune to an attack of stupid. Take Billy the Kid, asking *"Quien es?"* into a darkened room and absorbing Pat Garrett's bullet in answer to his question.

Or the nitwits who pulled the Roy's Branch train holdup near St. Joseph, Missouri, back in 1893. The three original members of the gang had recruited three more men for the job—their mistake was in taking the new guys at face value: One was a cop, and the other two were private citizens working with the police.

When the three real outlaws pushed into the express car, they were surprised to find it inconveniently full of policemen, who promptly blew two of them away. The third gang member was wounded but got clear—until he was caught the next day. He of course asserted his innocence, but he convinced nobody. Not only were there three honest men to identify him for what he was, but he had a bloody mess where three fingers used to be and a pocket full of cartridges to boot.

The Dalton Boys' disaster at Coffeyville is told in another chapter, but it typifies the horseback bandit at his worst. So does the chapter on trains and stagecoaches, and those on a couple of notorious gangs, like the Cooks and the Bucks. Their stock in trade was pure violence, intimidation, murder. There wasn't anything good to say about them, in spite of the innumerable books and articles extolling their daring.

Chapter 3

PSYCHOPATH

Bob Rogers

MANY OF THE OLD WEST'S outlaws may have been psychotic. Certainly that word aptly describes men like Rufus Buck, despicable rapist and murderer. But the worst of the crazies may have been a little-known outlaw called Bob Rogers.

One account of Rogers' brief and unpleasant existence tells that he was an impressionable punk who idolized the Dalton Gang and set out to emulate them sometime in 1892. Maybe he did worship at the Dalton shrine. If he did, though, the abrupt termination of his role models in Coffeyville clearly did nothing to make him alter his course.

He started small, like most of the criminals of that day. It was horse theft to begin with. He lifted about a dozen of somebody else's animals in Indian Territory, drove his booty over into Arkansas, and sold them. He didn't get away with it, and Deputy Marshal Heck Bruner duly dragged him back to Fort Smith to face Judge Isaac Parker, unfairly called the Hanging Judge.

Parker was even-handed, and he could be deeply merciful when he thought the occasion justified it. Because of Rogers' youth—he was nineteen—Parker decided to be lenient in this, Rogers' first offense. He gave the young man a prison sentence, but suspended it and put Rogers on probation. It was a mistake.

During his customary sentencing lecture, Parker gave Rogers some good advice, as he often did with bad men who appeared before him. "This is your first offense, lad," the judge said kindly. "If you continue in this path of life, death may be the penalty." It was very good advice, but Rogers paid no attention at all and quickly returned to his burgeoning career of larceny. In the fall of 1891, he was charged with assault with intent to kill a lawman, but released on bond.

He does not seem to have been tried for this offense, and for a time he remained just a small-time thief. But then, on November 3, he showed his true colors. It happened in Catoosa, when he met Jess Elliot. Elliot was a lawyer and Cherokee constable, and he was in town to serve some sort of legal process. He ended up in a Catoosa saloon, and there he met Bob Rogers. It is not recorded whether the two had ever met before, but they soon locked horns. Both men had been drinking, and John Barleycorn took his usual toll.

Whatever their falling-out was, it escalated into a fistfight, which Rogers clearly won. With Elliot on the saloon floor, other men stopped the fight. Rogers left, and Elliot was persuaded to stay in the bar and recuperate until he could ride. Elliot rested up a little; then he went outside, mounted, and rode off. So far, so good.

He did not get far, for Rogers was waiting for him. He charged into the constable and knocked him out of the saddle, then dismounted and drew his knife. As a contemporary account put it, Rogers "cut his throat with a knife, making three horrible gashes, and left him in the roadway."

Elliot bled to death in less than half an hour, as citizens, including a doctor, tried to save him. When he was gone, they stayed with the body, building a fire and sending one of their number to fetch Deputy Marshal John Taylor.

But before Taylor could reach them, Rogers suddenly appeared out of the night. While the horrified townsmen looked on, Rogers rode through the fire and ran off the good Samaritans. Then he took time to kick and stomp the lifeless body of his victim, put on and wore Elliot's hat for a while, rummaged through the constable's papers, and finally vanished into the night.

Marshal Taylor trailed Rogers as far as Sapulpa, but here the trail went cold. After his ghastly outrage against Elliot, nobody could doubt that Rogers had a crazy streak. And he would be back.

When Rogers returned, he had his own little gang, scum nearly as bad as he was. Two of them were the brothers grandly named Kiowa and Dynamite Jack Turner, the latter already wanted for murder up in Colorado. The other hoodlums were Willis Brown and one Bob Stiteler. The gang struck out to emulate the Daltons, and for a little while their criminal career went reasonably well.

In a period of two months, they managed two successful robberies, one on the Katy railroad line and a second on the Kansas and Arkansas Valley road at a place called Seminole Switch. They hit a bank, too, at Mound Valley up in Labette County, Kansas. It was a good beginning. Just before Christmas of 1893, they tried on a Katy train north of Vinita, but the engineer put the hammer down and dashed through the outlaws' ambush. Frustrated, the gang opened fire on the train, hitting the fireman in the jaw. But their bonanza was long gone.

On the same day, however, they managed to get this business of train robbery right. This time it was an Arkansas Valley train, which the gang successfully diverted onto a siding crowded with freight cars. The boys must have figured that their luck was in again. And so it was, however temporarily.

Things had started well for the gang, but early on, Rogers made a typical tyro outlaw mistake. He and Stiteler incautiously paid a visit to Rogers' brother-in-law, Henry Daniels. There they in turn were visited by the law in the person of Deputy Marshal W.C. Smith. Rogers was warming his feet before Daniels' fire and looked up to see the bad end of Smith's revolver. The officer sent Rogers' brother-in-law upstairs to bring Stiteler down, and Stiteler was forthwith arrested. So far, so good.

But before Smith could get his quarry out of the house, Rogers hit him in the head and he and Stiteler disappeared into the night. The law went to hunting, and the unfortunate Stiteler was back in custody before daybreak, but Rogers was gone. The officers pressed on with their search.

In January 1894 veteran marshal Heck Bruner led a posse to the gang's overnight camp on Big Creek. Caught by surprise, the gang came in a bad second. Kiowa was killed and Brown was badly wounded, hurt so badly that he would die at Vinita on the return trip to Fort Smith. Dynamite Jack, for all his ferocious name, surrendered. But once again Rogers was gone. There is a tale that Rogers had sold out his companions to the law in return for part of the reward money. Maybe so. Such treachery was surely not beyond Rogers' demonstrated depravity.

Early in 1895 Rogers seems to have tried his hand at running booze into Indian Territory, a federal offense. Warrants were also issued for him on charges of robbing two men, C.W. Adams and William Wiley. Rogers' fortunes had sunk very low by now. He was a flash in the pan, for the Wiley stickup netted the outlaw precisely three dollars. And at last he ran out of luck altogether, just a week after the robbery of Wiley.

Rogers had been elusive for a long time, but he could not run forever, not with the expert hounds of the Marshals Service baying on his trail. And so at last the law caught up with him on March 13, 1895. He was staying overnight with his father—another stupid mistake—in the elder Rogers' house at a place called Horseshoe Mound.

Ironically, the place was only some twenty miles south of Coffeyville, Kansas, scene of the Dalton Gang's disaster less than three years before. After midnight a large posse led by Deputy Marshal Jim Mayes stashed its horses in a thicket and surrounded the Rogers house. Once his men were in position, Mayes and eight other men approached the front of the building.

The elder Rogers appeared on the porch to ask what they wanted, and Mayes told him bluntly, "We want your son. The house is surrounded and he can't escape this time. Light a lamp." Rogers' father had no choice but to follow Mayes' orders, and the posse entered. Inside they found a couple named Collier, who worked for Rogers, but their quarry was upstairs. "Come down, Bob," Marshal Mayes called, "and surrender."

The reply was vintage Rogers. "Come and get me."

And so three of the lawmen went up the stairs to bring Rogers down, led by Deputy Marshal W.C. Daniels. About this time the Colliers, dressed in their nightclothes, ran into the night, sensing what was coming. They were wise.

Rogers met the three deputies at the head of the stairs. He had a revolver in each hand, but Daniels bravely challenged him. "Drop those guns," he said, and a sane, sensible man probably would have done just that. But this was Bob Rogers, who apparently was neither sane nor sensible, and he opened fire on the lawmen point-blank.

Daniels went down immediately with a bullet through the heart, and a second deputy, Phil Williams, took a serious arm wound. Williams fell backward into the third lawman, and the two tumbled together back down the stairs. Their fall may well have saved their lives.

The rest of the lawmen opened a furious fire on the house, driving something between two hundred and three hundred rounds through the board walls of the building. The bombardment continued until the house was riddled with holes and some of the rafters were virtually cut in two, but Rogers was still unhurt. The posse then sent the elder Rogers into the house to summon his son to surrender, but Rogers would not listen, even to his father. He defiantly retorted, "I'll give up after I am killed." Mayes' response was still more rifle fire, but Rogers remained miraculously unwounded, though his father is said to have been wounded in the big toe, of all places.

But then Rogers called out to the possemen, making a bizarre offer to surrender "if you let me bring my gun."

Doubtless this dubious offer must have sounded risky to Mayes and his men, but it was better than trying to send anybody back up those deadly stairs. Mayes agreed that Rogers could bring his rifle with him but cautioned the outlaw to keep the muzzle of the weapon depressed.

Lacking the slightest trust in Rogers, the marshal and his men sensibly took cover behind a stack of poles in the yard and waited for Rogers to appear. When their quarry walked out the door, Mayes stood up behind the poles. Rogers stopped and asked a strange question: "Do you have a warrant for me?" "No," said the marshal, "we don't need one."

At this Rogers raised the muzzle of the Winchester, but this time he never got off a shot. The whole posse opened up on him together, and Rogers went down full of holes. According to one account of the fight, Rogers had been hit by twenty-two bullets and two shotgun loads.

All of eastern Oklahoma could sleep more soundly.

Chapter 4

A QUIET DAY IN BRAGGS

The Verðigris Kið

HIS REAL NAME WAS Sam McWilliams, but he called himself the Verdigris Kid. Fancy handles like that weren't uncommon in the West. It wasn't at all unusual for an unprepossessing punk to try to inflate his image by inventing a tough-sounding nickname for himself.

No doubt these thugs thought a glamorous handle would make them something more than the insignificant hoodlums they really were. It was a vain hope, because most of them were pretty ordinary people, and some were downright stupid. In the end, of course, the great majority ended up permanently dead very early in life, or looking forward to many years of eating beans and viewing the world through a set of iron bars.

Which brings us to young Sam McWilliams, yclept the Verdigris Kid. The Verdigris River winds down out of eastern Kansas past Coffeyville, where the Daltons lost a shoot-out with a bunch of tough citizens. Then it wends its way on to its confluence with the broad Arkansas, down in Oklahoma. Just how McWilliams acquired his Verdigris Kid handle is lost in the mists of time, but maybe people started calling him that because his family lived along the Verdigris River.

Or maybe he acquired his handle simply by inventing himself—either way, that was the name Sam McWilliams died with. He came to his untimely and well-deserved end in the process of trying to push honest people around, the same thing he had done a good many times before. But this time the Verdigris Kid and some outlaw friends picked on the wrong town. They should not have ridden into the little Indian Territory settlement called Braggs, on the twenty-eighth of March, 1895.

Braggs was a bustling little settlement about nine miles east of Fort Gibson, not far from Muskogee. The settlement was named for one Solomon Bragg, a white man who settled in the Illinois District of the Cherokee Nation and married a Cherokee woman. Bragg built a grist mill, essential to an infant farm town trying to grow. Later on, the Iron Mountain Railway pushed its line down the Arkansas Valley and called its local stop Bragg Station.

In 1886 Braggs, as it had come to be called, got its own post office, which was set up, after the custom of the day, in John Patrick's store. Tom Madden founded a second store, and the town grew to include, besides the grist mill, a doctor's office, more shops, a feed store, and a lumberyard. The citizens added a blacksmith's shop, a hotel and a small bank, a grocery, a one-room school, and the Methodist church, served from time to time by itinerant preachers.

Today Braggs is as quiet a place as one can imagine, a sleepy wide spot in the road. But back in the nineteenth century it was very different. In common with a number of other little communities in Indian Territory, Braggs was a wild town in the first years of its life. In the early days the store windows were shuttered every night, it being the "habit of drunken horsemen to come into town at night to shoot out the lights seen through windows."

And there were other hazards for peaceful people. As one family sat at dinner in their log house, their eldest son, his back to the open door of the cabin, was killed by a bullet from outside the house. It came from a hoodlum who "mistook him for his father, a Texas white man who came there in early days and married a Cherokee woman." Store owner Tom Madden, a Cherokee, also had enemies to fear, so much so that he carried a gun in an innocuous paper bag. There had, said the *Muskogee Phoenix*, "been bad blood between Madden and certain other parties at Braggs for some time and that there would be bloodshed was not unexpected." The violence finally erupted in April 1896, and Madden either didn't have his paper bag with him or couldn't reach inside it in time. He was shot down in front of his store in the middle of the morning.

Such were the hazards of ordinary life in Indian Territory, and especially in little Braggs. To these dangers was added the constant threat of invasion by the plague of outlaws who infested the whole Territory. The *Fort Smith Weekly Elevator* reported that the

> "Bad men" had full sway for a time, robbing trains, looting express and post offices and pilliging [*sic*] stores, but after a while their actions became a stench in the nostrils of Uncle Sam, and the Government took a hand in the suppression of these highway robbers.

The reference was mostly to the infamous Cook Gang, who rivaled the vile Bucks as the worst scum ever to ride the Owl Hoot Trail in Indian Territory. Most of the gang had been run to earth, when in 1895 the Verdigris Kid rode into Braggs in company with Sam Butler and George Sanders, outlaws as bad as he was.

Sanders was also a leftover from the Cook Gang. That venomous bunch had included a rich collection of thugs, not least of which was multiple murderer Crawford Goldsby, called Cherokee Bill.

McWilliams, the Verdigris Kid, had started his criminal career in a humble way, by stealing three cows from a settler. He soon graduated to greater things, allying himself with the Cook Gang as they terrorized eastern Indian Territory. There he made himself a reputation of sorts: The Verdigris Kid would steal from anybody, individual people, banks, post offices, stages, and trains.

McWilliams was also part of a gunfight with a deputy marshal's posse out on the Caney River in northeastern Indian Territory, a fracas in which he took a bullet in the leg. He was treated by Dr. David Reece of Braggs, but he was, as will appear, most ungrateful.

He was also reputed to have backed Cherokee Bill in a robbery of the Schufeldt store in little Lenapah in the autumn of 1894. It was during that holdup that Cherokee Bill wantonly murdered an inoffensive citizen who did no more than look at the outlaws from outside the store window while the robbery was in progress. It was this pointless killing that would ultimately get Cherokee Bill well and truly hung at Fort Smith.

Thus the Verdigris Kid, a hoodlum without, as the judges say, any redeeming social value whatever. Sanders was an equally nasty piece of work. He had, as the *Eufaula Indian Journal* said with some contempt, "always been a desperado, though he only lately joined McWilliams":

> Last fall he robbed U.S. Drake at McKay by holding a revolver at his babe's head and threatening to kill it if he did not give up money. He was a brother of Levi Sanders who robbed the Fort Gibson mail hack, killed a woman, was himself killed near Tahlequah last summer.

Another territorial paper commented that "Sanders was a Cherokee murderer and has a bloody record."

Now it was March 1895, and a band of outlaws came riding into little Braggs. The old Cook Gang was no more, but Sam McWilliams and Sanders hadn't learned a thing from the end of their companions. On this day the gang included the Verdigris Kid, Sanders, and Butler, and there may have been others in the group as well.

They headed for the store run by Tom Madden, herding ahead of them whatever male citizens they encountered. Along with the other residents they stuck up and disarmed lawman Ed Barbee, who did not recognize the riders as outlaws until he was looking down their gun barrels.

Dismounting, McWilliams and Sanders pushed inside Madden's store, and there they helped themselves to whatever took their fancy. They would make a leisurely job of robbing the store and then rob the storekeeper when he arrived for the day's business.

Butler posted himself out in front of the store to intercept anybody wanting to go inside. He held at bay Barbee and several citizens collected on the way to Madden's store and herded together in front of it.

There was no resistance by the townsmen, caught unaware. Nevertheless, at some time during the robbery, an unarmed man was shot down. The *Edmond Sun-Democrat* reported somewhat obscurely that "the clerk, a young white man and son of the depot agent at Braggs, started to run out at the back door and were shot by the outlaws." This reference is almost surely to young Joe Morris, a clerk at Madden's, son of the railroad agent at Braggs.

However, as the pistol-waving Butler swaggered in the street and his comrades dallied inside the store, help for the town was on the way. Madden lived within sight of his store and was alarmed when through his spyglass he saw people standing on the store porch with their hands raised.

With more courage than sense, he wanted to leave his house and "make a fight of it himself," but his wife's cooler head prevailed. She "insisted that he go after the officers, who lived about a mile away," and Madden finally took her advice and used his horse instead of his gun.

The officers he found were a pair of tough Cherokee deputy sheriffs, Johnson Manning and Hiram Stevens (or Stephens), and the two lawmen hurried toward the town. Even with a mile to travel, they were in plenty of time, for the Verdigris Kid and Sanders were in no hurry about robbing Madden's place, apparently fully enjoying playing the role of big-time outlaws.

Not content with stealing whatever money Madden may have had in the till, they spent as long as forty minutes decorating themselves inside the store. "They removed their old shoes and put on new boots," said the *Weekly Elevator*, and

> new clothes and a large number of silk handkerchiefs were
> selected. One of the bystanders was made to lead up a fine
> road [*sic*] horse that was hitched in the street, unsaddle one

of the roan horses belonging to the robbers, and place the saddle on the roan.

The *Indian Journal* added dryly that the two outlaws

took things leisurely and picked out such goods as they wanted. Each had a suit apiece, and the two inside were picking out gloves when Butler warned them of the approach of Johnson Manning and Hiram Stevens.

Their posturing and preening abruptly ended, McWilliams and Sanders ran to the door of Madden's store and opened fire on the lawmen, killing Manning's horse. Manning and Stevens returned fire, and their shooting was deadly. The Verdigris Kid went down for keeps, shot through the center of the chest. He was just nineteen.

Lawman Barbee, disarmed by the outlaws, ran through the line of fire between them and the deputy sheriffs to snatch up McWilliams' Winchester and get into the fight. It was probably at this point that Madden's clerk, Joe Morris, courageously tried to help capture Sanders and Butler—maybe by running for the depot. He was shot through the body for his pains and fell, mortally wounded.

What followed was a monumental gunfight, as the surviving outlaws tried to hold off not only the deputies but a growing number of townspeople, armed and angry. In addition to Manning and Stevens, the early shooting was done by a merchant named Craig and a citizen called Ellis Petit. At the start of the fight, the outlaws sheltered behind one of their horses, but Petit dropped the horse, leaving the bandits exposed to a heavy and burgeoning hail of lead.

A man called G.W. Slater, a citizen who lived north of Braggs, had been pushing cattle that morning with a cowboy named Jim Green. Slater and Green had ridden into town to get something to eat and had settled themselves comfortably in the dining room of the town's little hotel just before the war started in the street outside.

Stray rounds from the beginning of the gun battle seriously discommoded the two diners, blasting the dishes from their table, and both men ran from the hotel. They sought out and quickly found what Slater thought was a deputy U.S. marshal—although Slater called the lawman Hiram Stephens. Their lunch destroyed, Slater and Green forthwith volunteered to "help capture the outlaws," a task which would turn out to be somewhat easier said than done. As Slater told the story years later, in the twilight of his life:

> We went behind the hotel and took our places at the corner
> of the building. One of the gang started around the corner
> and we shot him and his horse. This started a real battle.
> Other citizens came to our assistance and after a thirty minute
> battle we had killed all but one. He was trying to get out
> of town and was shooting back toward us. I had no more
> ammunition, so I picked up a gun belonging to one of the
> gang. . . . Butler's gun fell from his hands and he rode away
> speedily.

Up to this point Slater's personal account squares at least generally with other stories of the fight, but then it departs into the golden realm of hyperbole, painting the gunfight in the vivid colors of the Battle of Waterloo. "At the end of the battle," said this citizen much later, "there were thirteen dead men and twenty-seven dead horses. Those were very exciting days."

Exciting days indeed, no doubt. But it would appear that the Braggs fight got even more exciting as it ripened with time in Slater's memory. In fact, there is no certainty that more than two criminals died in the shoot-out in front of Madden's store, although some other recollections by area pioneers do indeed suggest that the outlaw casualty list may have been much higher.

One early settler named Albert Barry much later recalled a report that "five of the outlaws had been killed." Earlier that day, Barry said, he had sold ammunition to two men in a store at a settlement called Illinois Station. Barry took a train to Braggs after hearing of the fight there, "to find the dead were lying on the station platform. The first two I saw were the men I had sold the ammunition to . . . the only one I personally knew was Sam McWilliams, known as the Verdigris Kid."

However many outlaws were really involved in the Braggs gunfight, there were too many tough lawmen and pugnacious citizens for the bandits to cope with. With McWilliams down, Sanders and Butler—with any other gang members who may have been along and still breathing—fell back toward their horses, firing desperately at a growing host of enemies. Sanders didn't make it. Hit several times in the body and once in the temple, he went down for keeps in the dusty street of Braggs.

Butler managed to scramble to his horse through a hail of bullets and left Braggs at the high lope. Butler, according to the *Indian Journal*, "was thought to be wounded"; the *Weekly Elevator* asserted that he was hurt badly enough that he left a blood trail. Butler managed to elude pursuit, at least for the moment, but he did not have the sense either to put a lot of miles behind him in a hurry, or, as we shall see, to stay away from his own familiar haunts.

The remains of Sanders and the Verdigris Kid were tossed in a wagon and hauled off to Eufaula, where Bill Cook, McWilliams' erstwhile leader, was then languishing in jail. Officers brought the outlaw from his cell to view the corpses, and Cook, "laying his hand affectionately upon the box where his former comrade lay, said 'This is the Kid.'"

Thereafter, the remains were hauled off to Fort Smith and delivered to U.S. Marshal George J. Crump, "in order," wrote the *Beaver Herald*, "that the government reward of $250 for the body of 'Verdigris' might be collected." It is not recorded that the remains of Sanders were worth anything at all.

The *Herald* reported that a pistol found on McWilliams had been taken from a lawman killed during a train robbery at a place called Coretta. And as it turned out, when what was left of McWilliams and Sanders arrived in Fort Smith, one Buz (or Bass) Lucky was even then on trial there for his participation in that same Coretta robbery.

"He was," as the paper reported, "convicted an hour later." And the writer of the article concluded with some satisfaction, "These are the last of the outlaws who became famous as bandits in this section last year. All the balance have been killed or captured."

The good citizens of the Territory heard of the demise of the outlaws with considerable pleasure and satisfaction. One paper reported that the Verdigris Kid was "the last and one of the most desperate of the late Cook gang and has continued to terrorize the territory since Cook's capture."

With obvious happiness a government inspector named Johnston told the Eufaula newspaper, the *Indian Journal*, that "every man who was ever connected with the Bill Cook combination has now been accounted for to the satisfaction of the Government's officers, Verdigris Kid being the last one on the list."

This left only the verminous Butler, who proceeded to prove that, like most of his fellow outlaws, he was terminally stupid. Once he got clear of the town of Braggs, he simply rode on home, leaving a reasonably clear trail behind him. And so, on the night of August 1, 1895, Deputy Marshal John Davis followed Butler's track to what was then called the "Henry Chambers place," up on the Verdigris River. There lived both Butler's wife and his mother, and there, sure enough, was Butler also.

Butler was taking his ease beneath an apple tree, but he was awake, and when he saw Davis approaching, he jumped to his feet, grabbed his gun, and fired, driving a bullet through the lawman's right side.

Davis fell from his horse, mortally wounded, but his return fire smashed into Butler's chest and killed him instantly. Marshal Davis lived only about an hour after the fight, but at least he had the satisfaction of leaving the world a cleaner place.

Such was the great Braggs gunfight. Another account of the battle—without quoting sources—ends the tale of the Verdigris Kid in a different way. In this version the outlaws got away with their robbery at Braggs, at least temporarily. However, they were tracked by Hiram Stevens into the "mountain fastnesses along the

Arkansas." And there, this tale tells us, Stevens killed both Sanders and the Verdigris Kid when they resisted arrest. Butler then "took to the murky waters of the Arkansas and swam for his life. He has never been heard from since."

The reader may choose between these two satisfying endings, although the first version has substantial support from contemporary newspaper accounts. In either case the Territory had much reason to thank a couple of tough Cherokee deputies, a fearless lawman, and a bunch of angry citizens.

Chapter 5

A RICH COLLECTION OF TRASH

The Cook Gang

LIKE MOST WESTERN OUTLAW gangs, the Cooks were a gaggle of losers, banded together to steal what honest people earned, quite willing to kill any poor soul who got in their way. For sheer meanness, their only close rivals were the vicious Bucks, about whom more in another chapter.

The Cooks never partook of the sort of lasting notoriety showered on other gangs, equally contemptible but a bit more colorful. The James-Younger Gang, for example, was permanently enshrined by contemporary hyperbole and turned into folk heroes on the silver screen in dozens of mostly very bad movies. *Jesse James Meets Frankenstein's Daughter* was a particularly ugly example of the sort of awfulness Hollywood produced to capitalize on the names of famous outlaws.

The overrated Daltons also reaped reams of more or less accurate, usually florid prose that glorified them and turned them too into folk icons of a sort. *The Dalton Women* was only one of the multitude of movies that capitalized on a famous—or infamous—name, albeit one of the worst of the films about the gang.

Bill Cook.

But at least the Daltons and their ilk had panache of a sort, a sort of backward glamour in the public eye. Not the Cooks: no glamour here, no panache, just pure evil. Like most of the outlaws of the time, most of them ended up dead early in life. But while they lasted, they were a plague to honest men and women trying to make a life for themselves in Indian Territory. The newspapers of the time wrote about them as they would the Antichrist, and with good reason.

Deputy U.S. marshals, citizen posses, and Indian Lighthorse police chased them all over the eastern part of the Territory. In time even the Texas Rangers took their share in the hunt, which extended all the way from the Arkansas line into faraway New Mexico. Appeals were even heard for intervention by the U.S. Army to reinforce the marshals.

They were named after their leader, William Tuttle Cook, called Bill. The gang's heyday was the mid-1890s, and for a time they were such a pestilence that men—and women—feared to travel the roads and paths of the eastern Territory even in broad daylight. The Cooks were a sort of equal opportunity outlaw gang: They robbed anybody of anything and made no distinction between rich and poor; male and female; Indian, black, and white.

Inevitably, like nearly all the others of their ilk, the gang members came to the close of their brief careers in violence, dying full of lawmen's bullets or on the formidable gallows at Fort Smith. While some of their relatives may have shed a tear or two, the good citizens of Indian Territory rejoiced exceedingly at the termination of this bunch of arrogant bullies. The gang often committed their depredations in twos and threes, but from time to time they got together to rob as a group. Their cast of characters changed as outlaws joined, departed, or ended up dead, but the gang remained.

Bill Cook was one-eighth Cherokee, growing up over on the Neosho River north of Fort Gibson. His first brush with the law was a charge of selling whiskey, a federal offense in Indian Territory. He could have stopped there, but he didn't. For a while he punched cattle, and he even worked as a posseman for federal deputy marshal Will Smith.

But in 1894 his kid brother Jim was charged with larceny and compounded the problem by jumping bail. Bill joined him, a demonstration of his proclivity for the wrong side of the law. The two soon joined forces with a long-time acquaintance, one Crawford Goldsby, a vicious career outlaw by any standard.

Goldsby was a handsome young man of mixed blood, in various proportions Cherokee, Sioux, white, black, and Mexican. Deserted by his father, ignored by a stepfather, cordially disliked by his elder sister's husband, Mose Brown, he grew up wild. He rejoiced in an exotic handle acquired someplace early in life. He was called Cherokee Bill, a title maybe self-invented.

In 1892 he was hanging around the town of Catoosa, working in a livery stable and at whatever else came his way. He could not have been content with this workaday, law-abiding existence.

In those days Catoosa was a wild and woolly settlement, a railhead town that received some of the trail herds out of Texas. From Catoosa the cattle were shipped on farther north and east by train. With the cattle came the cowboys, young, full of beans, hungry for whiskey and the pleasures of the bedroom, "ready for a fight or a frolic," as the saying went. There was an ocean of whiskey and plenty of willing ladies in Catoosa. Trouble was also easy to find on its streets and in its saloons. It was Cherokee Bill's kind of town.

In Catoosa Bill met a couple of charter members of the gang. Thurman "Skeeter" Baldwin was a cowboy in his mid-twenties. Sam McWilliams was a seventeen-year-old wannabe rustler who answered to the moniker Verdigris Kid or Mosquita.

Toward the end of 1893, Goldsby got into big-time trouble with the law. He was attending a dance down in Fort Gibson and got into a quarrel over a girl with whom he was enamored, no doubt fueled by whiskey. The end of it was a fistfight in which Cherokee Bill was decisively pummeled by a freedman named Jake Lewis.

Goldsby was not designed to call his defeat a lesson learned and move on, and so the next day he renewed the fight. But this time there was no challenge or struggle and there were no fists; he simply ambushed his rival in a stable and drove two pistol bullets into Lewis. Lewis survived, but Cherokee Bill did not wait around to discuss the rights and wrongs of the incident. Instead, he prudently went "on the scout," as the saying went, and joined up with Bill Cook and his brother Jim, the Verdigris Kid, Skeeter Baldwin, and some other equally worthless hoodlums. The gang went off stealing horses and watching their back trail for lawmen or irate ranchers. Bill would be hard to catch, since he knew "nearly every pigtrail of the Indian Territory."

A fairy tale about Bill related that he could "burst a squirrel's eye, as far as he could see, every shot," and this with iron sights, no less. Although this is an obvious piece of overblown hyperbole, it speaks volumes about Cherokee Bill's local reputation as a marksman.

Friends talked to Bill and urged him to surrender. It was a logical and prudent notion because both he and Lewis were Cherokee freedmen, the Cherokee court had jurisdiction, and the sentence would probably be relatively light. Goldsby elected to stay on the run.

And then, in the spring of 1894, came the payment of the United States subsidy or "Strip Money," almost seven million dollars to be paid to members of the Cherokee Nation gathered at Tahlequah. The payments—an enormous amount of money in one place—attracted all sort of other people like moths to a flame.

Besides legitimate businessmen, Tahlequah swarmed with snake-oil salesmen, gamblers, whiskey sellers, thieves, a man who ran a steam-driven merry-go-round, and an assortment of feather merchants offering all manner of desirable items on credit.

Violence inevitably followed, violence great and small. Among the more serious offenses were a stage holdup and the murder of an inoffensive woman by one Levi Sanders, who was promptly shot quite dead by his victim's son.

As Cherokees, Goldsby and the two Cook boys were entitled to payments at Tahlequah, but being sought by the law presented some difficulty to collecting in person. So they gave written permission to a woman called Effie Crittenden to collect their shares. A

Cherokee posse got wind of this and rode off to Effie's home to collect the outlaws. In the gunfight that followed, Effie prudently crawled behind the cookstove while the bullets flew. Either Goldsby or one of the Cooks killed posse member Sequoyah Houston, a respected full-blood member of the Cherokee police, called the Lighthorse.

The outlaws escaped, maybe because, according to legend, their sister, called Lou or Ludy, saddled their horses for them as they fought off the law. They got away all right, but they did not escape unscathed. Jim Cook carried eight buckshot in his body, and here legend first rears its head. The story goes that Effie, asked if Goldsby was part of the outlaw gang, said, "No. It was Cherokee Bill." It's a nice story, but in all probability Goldsby had carried his famous handle long before this bloody day.

Now the pursuit was joined by an angry group of Houston's relatives and friends, while Jim Cook got his wounds patched up at gunpoint. The other outlaws threatened the good Samaritan, a doctor named Howard, with death if he told anybody that they had visited him, but the three were seen crossing the Arkansas on a ferry.

A gunfight followed between Cherokee Bill and Deputy U.S. Marshal John McGill. Neither man was hurt, and the two unwounded outlaws fled when McGill was reinforced. Jim Cook couldn't run, however, and was captured, as the Muskogee *Indian Journal* put it, "shot as nearly to pieces as it is possible to be and live." He was held to be tried for murder by the Cherokee tribal court at Tahlequah.

Now Cook and Goldsby were wanted men, and with any sense at all they would have left Indian Territory altogether. But instead of fleeing, they made outlawry a full-time business. Setting out to make a career of oppressing the righteous, they attracted other worthless trash, including the aforementioned Verdigris Kid and Skeeter Baldwin.

To these they added other outlaws and would-be felons: Lon Gordon, Jess Snyder (called Buck), Elmer Lucas (known as Chicken), Curtis Dayson, Jim French, a killer called Buss (or Buz)

Luckey, George Sanders, and one Henry Munson, a penitentiary alumnus who dubbed himself Texas Jack Starr.

Sanders, brother to the late unlamented murderer Levi, was a particularly vicious sort, who once robbed a man by "holding a revolver at his baby's head and threatening to kill it if he did not give up his money." French had already tried to kill a couple of people and was also wanted for mail robbery.

This collection of hoodlums the papers soon called the Cook Gang, although its members committed their crimes in pairs and small bunches about as often as they got together to defy the law en masse. In July 1894, for example, Cherokee Bill and Jim French stuck up the general store in little Wetumka; in the same month Goldsby and Munson robbed Dick Richards, railroad station agent at Nowata. True to his salt, Richards went for his pistol, and Cherokee Bill shot him in the neck and killed him.

Less than a day later, six outlaws stopped the Muskogee–Fort Gibson stage and robbed the passengers. The holdup men wore masks, but the press concluded—probably correctly—that the evil-doers were members of the Cook Gang. About an hour after that, the same bunch robbed a well-known Cherokee man.

Still in July the train depot at Illinois was robbed once, the Fort Gibson depot twice, and a man from the hamlet of Muldrow murdered and robbed of about one thousand dollars. At midmonth a gang—this time certainly the Cooks—held up a Frisco train at a tiny place called Red Fork. This time the haul was meager indeed, for the gang got only a few dollars, a box of cigars, and a jug of whiskey. All of them were too dense to inspect the express agent's receipt book, into which he had stuffed a large amount of cash.

So far the gang's holdups had been easy, no doubt inflating their own opinions of themselves. But now all of that was about to change. At the end of July, they barged into the Lincoln County Bank in Chandler, only to find that the time lock on the bank's safe was still set. When a sick bank employee, ordered to open the safe, fainted from his illness, one of the frustrated outlaws took a shot at the man as he lay on the floor.

Their next mistake was both callous and stupid. They killed the popular town barber, shooting him down simply because he shouted that the bank was being robbed. The shot, far more likely than a yell to alert the town, brought a very tough sheriff called Claude Parker. Parker stood boldly in the middle of the street and emptied his pistol at the outlaws, hitting one horse and one man.

The gang stood not upon the order of their going from Chandler, and Parker raised a small posse and pursued. More shooting followed, and four miles or so out of town, the posse collected Chicken Lucas, shot in both legs, and probably displeased that the gang had not only galloped off and left him but also taken his horse. Yes, said he, it was the Cook Gang that did the deed. Exit Chicken, off to the lockup in Guthrie, where he would be safe from a mob of angry Chandler citizens.

Chicken kept on talking. The other robbers, he said, had been Bill Cook, Cherokee Bill, Gordon, and Munson, and he also helpfully volunteered the information that he had ridden along on the Red Fork train robbery.

The gang surfaced again on August 2, and on that day a tough band of Euchee Indians jumped them at the home of Munson's uncle. Warned of the approach of the Euchees, Cherokee Bill and Cook said they "didn't care a damn for all the Indians in the Territory."

They should have, for in the battle that followed Munson was killed and Curtis Dayson captured. Lon Gordon went down with a bullet through the lungs and died shortly afterward in Sapulpa. Only Cook, Snyder, Baldwin, and Cherokee Bill got away.

In early September Jim French and a man called Meigs decided to hold up one Robert Bean at his home near Tahlequah. They halted outside and "called Bean from his house." Bean obliged them by coming out, but the trouble was, he came smokin', as the saying goes. He shot Meigs in the chest and the outlaws fled empty-handed.

Then, on the night of September 14, Cook, Snyder, Baldwin, and Cherokee Bill rode into town at Okmulgee. Much of the town being conveniently absent watching a baseball game, they had little trouble robbing some six hundred dollars from the local store.

They next attacked the depot at Fort Gibson, where they got another three hundred dollars and galloped out of town spraying bullets. This time there were six in the gang, which included both French and the Verdigris Kid. The next day they robbed a lone traveler and then split up. Cook and two other outlaws then robbed a group of coal miners of whatever pittance they may have had.

But then they missed a real haul in Claremore, when the station agent was warned that suspicious-looking riders were coming into town. The agent prudently evacuated his funds on the outbound train, and the gang came away empty-handed. Twenty miles away at Choteau, the gang got a sack of silver and gold and silver certificates from the American Express agent. They also robbed a railroad employee of a measly thirty-five dollars. So much for Robin Hood.

Deputy U.S. Marshal Bill Smith was able to set up a meeting with Cook, a sort of parley, trying to get Cook to come in and surrender. It was too late, the outlaw said. He and the others were going to set up "in the robbing business for keeps."

By now the honest people of eastern Indian Territory had had a great bellyful of the Cooks. One politician told the *Kansas City Times* that "people are afraid to travel," which was surely understandable in view of the gang's propensity for robbing anybody and anything. One cable to Washington pleaded that "Affairs here are in a desperate condition; business is suspended, the people generally intimidated and private individuals robbed every day and night."

Even the residents of the little towns lived in fear. A Muskogee resident remembered a friend placing a six-gun on the table and commenting, "I understand the Cook gang is coming in tonight." The Muskogee merchants organized a home guard and installed an alarm system to alert the town's defenders.

According to the Fort Smith *Indian Journal*, U.S. Marshal George Crump offered a reward of $250 a head for Cook Gang members, dead or alive. His offer named, besides Cook and

Cherokee Bill, an astonishing number of wanted men, including Bill Doolin and the Slaughter Kid—a sobriquet of Bittercreek Newcomb—and a host of lesser lights.

Now the lawlessness got even worse. On October 20 the gang wrecked a Katy train at a town called Coretta, throwing a switch and sending the train smashing into a line of boxcars on the siding. Firing their weapons, presumably to cow the passengers, the gang robbed the express car of about five hundred dollars and then went through the train robbing individual passengers.

But the gang was frustrated by the stout "through safe" in the express car, for the keys to a through safe were kept only at the safe's final destination. Seeing another train coming, they "fired a last volley at the train and disappeared into the darkness." Two passengers were wounded, one of them seriously, and the train had been "riddled with bullets, every window being broken, even the steam gauge and gauge lamp being shot away."

Late in October a couple of gang members stopped a series of drummers traveling between Fort Gibson and Vinita. The haul was small again, which irritated the outlaws, according to the *Vinita Indian Chieftain*, into "roundly reprimanding" two of their victims for leaving their watches and most of their money elsewhere.

The gang sacked the tiny hamlet of Watova, robbing two stores and the post office. Not satisfied, they tried to stop a passing passenger train. With their usual acumen, however, they managed to throw the switch lever the wrong way, allowing the train to go charging past them, entirely unrobbed. The next day the whole gang passed the time holding up travelers on the Tahlequah–Fort Gibson road.

By this time the gang's depredations were badly hurting the economy of eastern Indian Territory. Travelers even left their money and watches at home whenever they could. Banks charged a premium for issuing sight drafts, which were instantly negotiable, Pacific Express suspended its money order business, many businesses closed at nightfall, and businessmen who had to move money concealed it in various ingenious ways. The *Oklahoma State Capital* reported that "one traveling man brought $3,000 out sealed in a horse collar; another drummer brought out $1,500 in the bottom of a sack of oats."

And the ravages of the gang went on unabated. They robbed still another depot, an attack preceded by a noisy demonstration in Fort Gibson. There, the story goes, the Cooks' stepsister Lou—or Ludy, or maybe Lulu—galloped into town and shot up the depot with her pistol. Lou was said to be attractive and given, like Belle Starr, to posturing with big horses and big pistols. The folklore of the gang says she was trying to draw attention away from the gang's foray.

But the omens were not good for the Cooks. Curtis Dayson and Chicken Lucas got, respectively, fifteen and ten years for the Red Fork attack. The tempestuous stepsister Lou got herself arrested on a charge of harboring outlaws, which no doubt she did. Still, things were so bad that the Indian agent at Muskogee wired Washington asking for military help to break what he called "the state of siege."

The gang's crimes were prime fodder for the many people who wanted all of Oklahoma made a state. Newspapers both in and out of the Territory clamored for statehood as the sovereign remedy for this crime wave. "How much longer," grumbled the *Afton Weekly Herald*, "is Bill Cook going to be allowed to terrorize the Indian Territory?"

Still not smart enough—or maybe too arrogant—to leave the Territory, the gang split up again and went right on with their crimes. Cook, Skeeter, Snyder, and one William Farris robbed a trading post on November 2, and two days later held up an emigrant family on the road.

The Verdigris Kid and Cherokee Bill rode into Lenapah town and went into the Schufeldt store, where they forced Schufeldt to open the safe. They cleaned it out and robbed the owner as well, stole some merchandise and ammunition, and held up the post office for good measure. And here tragedy struck, when a harmless man working next door looked into Schufeldt's from a window. Cherokee Bill wantonly killed him with a single rifle round.

The outlaws made a clean getaway, but the deputy marshals used an informer to locate the pair. A posse led by the formidable Heck Bruner and Heck Thomas found them at a house owned by one Frank Daniels, up on the Caney River. In the inevitable firefight that followed, somebody got a bullet into Cherokee Bill's leg and another bullet killed the Verdigris Kid's horse. Deputy Marshal Jim Carson was shot in the foot, but Cherokee Bill and McWilliams managed to get away.

A traveler who met the pair on the road told a newspaper that Cherokee Bill "says that he will die with his boots on and that some of the marshals will bite the dust too, when he does."

Anxiety mounted in Indian Territory, and petitions bearing five thousand signatures were sent to President Cleveland asking for help. Alarming rumors of the gang abounded, one of which credited the gang with "thirteen heavily armed men." More counties began to form their own home guards, but at the moment, had they but known it, part of the danger to honest people had already taken itself far away. For remorseless pursuit by Lighthorse riders and deputy marshals had at last driven Cook and four other outlaws across the Red River into Texas, where they intended to pass their time usefully, robbing trains. A suspicious rancher spotted them, however, and thoughtfully wired Company B of the Rangers at Amarillo.

Sergeant W.J.L. Sullivan—inevitably called John L.—collected five other Rangers and responded. The Rangers collared a mounted outlaw sentry without outcry and then surrounded the building where the gang was hiding.

There was an exchange of gunfire, but then the reports from the house fell away into silence. The Rangers broke down the door to find the bandits had fled to the attic. The lawmen heard one of the outlaws call out that he wanted to surrender, but then somebody else threatened to kill him if he did. Sergeant Sullivan quickly settled the question when he threatened to burn the house down and the gang with it. Cook had gotten away, but the other four gang members surrendered.

The prisoners, returned to Fort Smith, turned out to be Skeeter, Snyder, Farris, and a local recruit, Charles Turner. Skeeter got thirty years and Farris and Snyder both got twenty, which prompted Skeeter to comment with some bitterness, "What a hell of a court for a man to plead guilty in." Turner was acquitted.

The lessons of their trial were entirely lost on the rest of the gang. Jim French and three others rode into Checotah to rob the Lafayette Brothers store, but all they got was some merchandise and a paltry sum of money. On December 17 French tried to rob a store at Texana but was ignominiously driven off when the two clerks opened fire. Then, on Christmas Eve, Cherokee Bill led Jim French, Sanders, and the Verdigris Kid into the depot at Nowata, where they got almost two hundred dollars.

The next day the gang stopped the stage between Muskogee and Tahlequah and robbed the passengers. The papers reported that "all passengers were ruthlessly robbed, the ladies being even compelled to remove their shoes and turn their hose." That was certainly the grossest behavior, an abrupt and crude departure from the mores of the day. "If there was any chivalry about the highwaymen," one female passenger reported, "the ladies did not discover it."

Meanwhile, Cherokee Bill had gone to see his stepsister Maude Brown at Talala, and while he was there he got crossways with her husband Mose, with whom he had always had difficulty. When Mose threatened to talk to the law about Bill, or Bill thought he was going to, Cherokee Bill put seven Winchester bullets into Mose, whereof he died. Instead of running, Bill celebrated his latest murder by robbing the Kansas and Arkansas Valley depot at Nowata.

Bill Cook, on the run, still had the remorseless Sergeant Sullivan on his back trail. The Ranger followed reports of Cook all over west Texas and then followed his track clear into New Mexico. As Cook kept moving on, one sheriff after another got involved in the chase.

Cook got as far as Roswell, New Mexico, but on January 11, 1895, the law at last ran him down and took him without a fight. He was returned to Fort Smith, where tough Judge Isaac

Parker invited him to spend the next forty-five years in the prison in Albany, New York.

While Cook was hearing where he'd be living for the next many years, on March 28 Jim French and the Verdigris Kid stuck up a store in Fort Gibson, helping themselves not only to the available cash but to new suits and a variety of other clothing.

Meanwhile, Cherokee Bill, deeply enamored of a young lady named Maggie Glass, was determined to see her. And so he agreed to a rendezvous at the home of her older cousin, one-time deputy marshal Ike Rogers. Rogers had been discharged from the Marshals Service for conniving with outlaws, and his financial situation had deteriorated since that day. Now he earnestly wished reinstatement. U.S. Marshal George Crump promised Rogers that he would con-sider reinstatement if Rogers would help bring in Cherokee Bill. Rogers said he would.

So in early February 1895, Rogers enlisted a neighbor, Clint Scales, to help him lay Cherokee Bill by the heels and invited both Maggie and Bill to visit him. As always, Cherokee Bill was alert and wary; he did not trust Rogers at all. Neither, it turned out, did Maggie, who even urged Bill to leave the house. He would not leave and said ominously, "If Rogers makes a play, I'll show him how long it takes to commit murder."

So Bill stayed on at Rogers', his Winchester constantly on his knees. He refused a drink of whiskey, which Rogers had thought-fully spiked with morphine, and the men played cards most of the night. When they finally turned in at about four a.m., Rogers shared a bed with Bill, but each time Rogers moved Bill did also.

It was not until after breakfast the next morning that Rogers got his chance. When Bill rolled a cigarette and reached down to the fireplace for a coal to light it with, Rogers bashed him in the head with chunk of wood, or maybe it was the fire poker, depending on what account you read. A wild wrestling match followed, until Rogers and Scales finally subdued Cherokee Bill after a long struggle.

He was taken to Fort Smith, still the same arrogant braggart he had always been, boasting that if the deputy marshals "will just put me back on the prairie, I can whip any ten of them in the Territory." He would not get the chance, for he was tried in February 1895, and on April 13 Judge Parker sentenced him to hang for murder. He was well and truly hung on March 17, 1896. He had no last words, in spite of the oft-repeated fable that when asked whether he wanted to say something, he answered, "I came here to die, not to make a speech," or something like that.

With Cherokee Bill safely incarcerated, the next bandit to fall was Jim French, on a bitter cold day in February 1895. He had gone to Catoosa, this time with a new partner, one Jess Cochran, who called himself Kid Swanson and Slaughter Kid. They had decided to rob the Reynolds general store, and the neophyte Cochran botched the job by firing through the office door to gain admission and then charging through to collect the money.

What Cochran collected was a shotgun charge fired by clerk Tommy Watkins, who had been seated inside the office. The blast separated the outlaw from most of his head. Meanwhile, French fired through the window, mortally wounding the store manager, Sam Irwin, who was lying on a cot in the office.

Watkins missed French with his second barrel, leaving him at the bandit's mercy. Enraged at the shooting of Cochran, French was preparing to kill Watkins when the dying Irwin pulled a pistol from beneath his pillow and fired. He drilled French twice in the neck, and the outlaw staggered away from the building, all the fight gone out of him.

Leaving his guns behind, French managed to mount and ride to an old cabin about a mile away. As he hobbled through the front door, the residents vamoosed out the back, and in time a posse appeared, led by the formidable Watkins and his shotgun.

Nobody is sure exactly how French met his end. One version has French already permanently dead when the posse got there, one leg fallen in the fireplace and partially burned. Or, in another version reported by the *Muskogee Phoenix*, "a crowd followed to a cabin a half mile distant and filled him full of lead and laid him out and next day turned him under."

Or maybe, as the *Cherokee Advocate* reported, French lived long enough to look out the window of the shack at the approaching citizens, only to absorb a shotgun blast with his face, or maybe it was the back of his head.

However French departed this earth, he was gone for good, to the intense relief of the populace. Deputy Marshal Heck Thomas and a couple of citizens delivered what was left of him to Fort Smith, where his remains were placed on show for several hours after the custom of the time and viewed by "thousands of the curious." Learning of French's death from his jail cell, Bill Cook made a prophetic comment: "He's better off than we are," Cook said.

He was right.

Indian Territory rejoiced at the passing of the last of the Cook gang, but one ugly postscript remained. Friends of Cherokee Bill smuggled a pistol into the jail, and in July 1895 the outlaw killed respected guard Larry Keating in an attempt to break out. A firefight followed inside the jail, with Cherokee Bill shooting at anything that moved and screeching an unearthly war cry—"gobbling," men called it.

At last outlaw Henry Starr, also jailed there, talked Bill out of his revolver. He appealed to Bill's love for his mother, Starr said afterward. Bill was convicted of this murder as well and paid for his murders on the Fort Smith gallows.

The Verdigris Kid was still on the loose and should have been bright enough to put a lot of miles between him and Indian Territory. Predictably, as with so many of his profession, he hung around and went back to robbing. He would survive for a little while, until, that is, he chose to hoorah a little town near Muskogee, as related elsewhere.

The rest of the Cook Gang's brief history is largely sordid anticlimax. In the spring of 1897, Cherokee Bill's brother Clarence murdered Ike Rogers, captor of his brother; he got away and died much later in St. Louis of tuberculosis.

Jim Cook escaped from the Cherokee prison in December 1896. He recruited a couple of second-rate helpers and put on a largely unproductive minor crime wave. Jim died with his boots on, too, in 1900, shot down in an argument over the ownership of a steer. His brother Bill, who started the whole nefarious mess, died in prison in 1900.

Now all that remained of the gang were the bloody memories.

Chapter 6

THE EMPTY MEN

The Buck Gang

INDIAN TERRITORY WAS a tough land at the best of times. The *Muskogee Phoenix* told the tale of the Davis family, whose two sons were in the Fort Smith jail awaiting shipment to the penitentiary. The boys' mother and sister traveled to Fort Smith to say good-bye and were astonished—and presumably distressed—to find that husband and father Davis had gotten there before them, arrested and lodged in the same jail as his sons. But even in this rough-and-tumble land, the Buck Gang was something especially ugly.

They didn't have a long run, as outlaw careers went, but while they were at it the Buck Gang inspired a fear and disgust in the people of Indian Territory unmatched by any other gaggle of criminals. There is such a thing as pure evil in the world, and if you doubt it, follow the brief, ugly history of the Bucks.

What made the Buck Gang especially loathsome was that they were fond of committing the ultimate sin of the time: They were rapists. While murder and robbery and larceny were bad enough, and were all common offenses out beyond the Arkansas, rape was considered especially heinous, so much so that it carried the death penalty in Judge Parker's much-feared court at Fort Smith. The

Not so tough: the Buck Gang.

OKLAHOMA UNIVERSITY WESTERN HISTORY LIBRARY

Bucks indulged in some larceny, but they didn't seem especially interested in robbing trains or banks or stores. What they liked best was simply brutalizing people.

Had any of the real outlaws of Indian Territory been interviewed, they too would have had nothing good to say about the Buck Gang. Comments from, say, the Dalton Boys would have been along the lines of John Dillinger's famous remark about Bonnie and Clyde, that "they gave bank robbery a bad name."

The people of that day didn't spend a whole lot of time worrying about psychosis, and not at all about deep-seated childhood repressions and Oedipus complexes and the like. The chances are that nobody had heard of Sigmund Freud's theory of dreams out in the Territory, and they wouldn't have cared what the good doctor said in any case. The rape of a decent woman was right up there with the other unforgivable crimes: the murder of a child, a doctor, or a minister.

Rufus Buck was a Euchee Indian with a string of minor crimes behind him. He had done time in the pokey at Fort Smith, and now he was headed for the big time. Rufus had delusions of grandeur. He is said to have bragged about how he would lead a gang that would eclipse the criminal record of every other outlaw in the territory. In the end, however, he managed just thirteen days of lawlessness, a short career, but ugly enough while it lasted.

He led a band of young men as vile as he was. He started with Lewis and Lucky Davis—not related except in depravity—who were Creek freedmen, having both black and Indian blood. Later he would add Sam Sampson and Maoma July, both Creek Indians. Like Buck, all of them had criminal records and had spent some time in the Fort Smith jail.

All five proved to be unusually vicious, even for those violent times. They all turned out to be terminally stupid as well. And that is what ultimately got them hung at Fort Smith.

Buck was the son of a prominent Euchee politician, who either wouldn't or couldn't control his hoodlum son. Buck senior was a staunch advocate of Indian independence, and his son chose that theme to justify his crime wave. After one particularly vicious rape, he piously announced that in the future whites would "think ten times" before they took Indian land.

It is difficult to see the connection between the rape of a helpless woman and the quite legitimate desire of many Indians to govern themselves without interference from the federal government. Nevertheless, like terrorists everywhere, Rufus apparently felt a need to justify his crimes in the holy cause of Indian independence.

In the event, his ugly offenses angered the Indian population as much as it did the white. Within days he would have the Lighthorse, the Indian police, on his back trail as well as federal officers and angry citizens.

The gang started out small. They rustled twenty-three hogs and managed to sell them at a store in a tiny place called Orcutt, trading the critters for twenty-one dollars and a quantity of something called Hostetter's Bitters, apparently fond of the alcohol of which it was partly made. They next stole a blooded horse, later recovered. It wasn't much of a crime wave thus far, and Buck had to interrupt his new career to do a short stretch in the Fort Smith jail for bringing whiskey into Indian Territory.

And there Buck met his idol, Crawford Goldsby, better known as Cherokee Bill, a hoodlum entirely without redeeming social value, the sort of professional outlaw Buck aspired to be. While Buck was in the slam, Cherokee Bill tried to break out and in the process killed a highly respected jailer.

Having learned nothing from his stint behind bars, Buck was next pinched for something to do with rustling, having graduated from hogs to cattle. He did not stand trial this time, however, snatching his guard's semiautomatic pistol and running away down the streets of Okmulgee. He was ready for the big time and he had his gang formed, having added July and Sampson, both from the area of Tulsey—later Tulsa.

This time it was arson. Early in the morning of July 29, 1895 a fire raged through the little town of Checotah, on the Katy railroad southeast of Okmulgee. The fire had begun in the livery stable and rapidly spread, and the whole town turned out to fight the flames, including an itinerant fire-extinguisher salesman who promptly put his stock to work. The townspeople managed to save the horses from the fire, but the stable was ruined. Surveying the damage after the fire was out, the stable owner noticed that none of the ironwork of "some excellent saddles" could be found.

It then developed that somebody had stolen some fine horses from a nearby pasture and presumably had saddled them with the stolen horse furniture, setting fire to the stable to cover their crime. It was the Buck Gang, and worse was to come. Now it would be cold-blooded murder.

Another one of their crimes was the shooting of John Garrett, a black deputy U.S. marshal, near the town of Okmulgee on July 28, 1895. The story goes that the lawman was deliberately murdered because he knew the gang members for what they were. He had an alert eye on the five, knowing they were bad news and wondering what they were up to.

One well-researched account tells that Garrett was hunting for Buck and went to Peterson's store because Buck's mother was also there. As he went out to the back porch to see her, her son stepped out of hiding and shot him down; then Buck and the Davis boys mounted and galloped whooping out of town. According to another account, the marshal was called to a robbery in progress at Peterson's and made the mistake of ordering Rufus Buck to throw up his hands. Instead, Buck turned on the marshal and killed him.

Whether Buck alone murdered the lawman or other gang members helped him, their names would quickly become synonymous with unbridled ferocity, conduct much worse than that of the really famous gangs like the Daltons. For, having committed murder, what the gang tried next was a brutal rape.

They first encountered a wagon driven by a man named Ayers, and seated beside him was his daughter. These were the sort of odds Buck liked, and so he and his four henchmen stopped Ayers, ordered his daughter out of the wagon, and one by one raped her.

The *Muskogee Phoenix* reported that the girl received "critical injuries." If the murder of the lawman had not been enough, this crime put the gang beyond the pale for all time. Having amused themselves brutalizing Miss Ayers, the gang rode off for further adventures.

Next, on Berryhill Creek not far from Okmulgee, the five stopped and robbed a man called Jim Staley. Staley was riding a high-class horse, and Buck offered to trade him for the animal. When Staley said he wasn't interested, Buck struck him in the head with his Winchester and knocked him bleeding from the saddle. Then the gang pretty well cleaned poor Staley out, taking his watch, fifty dollars, and his fine horse and horse furniture. But at least they left him alive, after a debate and a vote over whether and how to kill him. The vote was three to two, and by that narrow margin Staley lived.

The next victim was Bert Callahan, owner of the U-Bar Ranch on Grave Creek. The gang jumped Callahan and his hired hand, a black cowboy named Sam Houston, while the pair was returning to the ranch from Okmulgee and opened fire without warning. Houston's horse was killed, and Houston ran for his life. Buck drove a bullet through Houston's lungs and then turned on Callahan, shooting a piece off one of his ears.

Buck had recognized Callahan as the son of the superintendent of Wealaka Mission School, from which Buck had been ejected for causing disturbances there. "If I'd known it was you," said Buck, "I'd have killed you too."

Cornered, Callahan lost everything *but* his life, even his clothes. He ran for his life down the road, bootless and naked, as the gang shot at him. An alternative version of the attack on Callahan calls his companion a young black boy, but agrees that the gang callously shot the youngster down. Since Houston was a black man, it is likely that both versions are close to the truth.

In either case, being bootless, it took Callahan some time to find help and get a wagon to haul out his companion. Houston lingered at death's door for a while, but he would survive. A posse went to the site of the ambush but could not pick up the outlaws' trail until daylight, August 5.

The gang's next crime was bungled. They tried a bit of nighttime horse thievery at Gus Chambers' home on Duck Creek in the area of Sapulpa. But Chambers was tough and he owned a shotgun, so what they got was not horses but gunfire, and the gang had to content themselves with riddling Chambers' house with bullets while the farmer's family cowered under a bed. The Bucks appear to have had no lack of ammunition, for about a hundred shots were fired in the fight, eight of which struck the bed under which the family had taken refuge.

On August 5 the gang stopped two wagons. One was driven by Mrs. Mary Wilson, a widow moving her possessions from one farm to another. With her was her son Charles and a boy she had hired to help out. After Buck and his minions took what they wanted from

Mrs. Wilson, they told the boys to drive on down the road. Lucky Davis then turned to the helpless woman. "Stand by, fellahs," he said; "watch how an expert makes love." After he had raped her, the gang drove her into the brush with gunfire, and there she was found by a posse "half dead from fright and abuse."

That was a Monday morning, and for the gang it would be a full day. During that evil day they robbed a man working on a ranch between Checotah and Okmulgee and murdered him. That night they went to a house where a schoolteacher was boarding, stuck up everybody there, and raped the teacher.

As if these outrages were not enough, on August 6 the Buck Gang reached a new level of depravity. They rode up to Henry Hassan's home between Snake and Duck Creeks, some twenty miles from Sapulpa. There they rode into the yard and asked for water. Hassan had been dozing under an arbor while his thirty-year-old wife, his mother-in-law, and his three small children peeled fruit nearby.

Hassan and Lewis Davis had had trouble before, when Hassan had asked him to close Hassan's gates after he passed through. Davis had replied in his typically arrogant way: "I got more important things to do; I ought to tear down the whole damn fence." Hassan recognized him now and knew he and his family were in the hands of the worst band of outlaws of the day. He tried to casually enter his house to get his Winchester, but Maoma July beat him to it.

Buck was his usual boastful self, bragging that he was Cherokee Bill's brother—which he was not—and demanded that Mrs. Hassan and her mother cook them a dinner and be damned quick about it. The gang ransacked the house, stealing what pittance of money Hassan had and other trinkets and articles of clothing, including, of all things, baby dresses. They then stuffed their bellies with dinner and afterward began to amuse themselves.

Lewis Davis began, forcing Mrs. Hassan to go to the barn. When she pleaded with him, he threatened to kill Hassan "and throw the God damn brats in the creek." The whole gang joined in, tied the lady down, and took turns raping her while those not engaged held Hassan prisoner.

Their lust satisfied, the gang turned on Hassan, whom they forced to ride with them to a field some two miles away. There they forced him to jump into a pool of water. One account says they knew Hassan had been a professional "buck and wing" dancer and so they forced him to dance, shooting at his heels to liven up their antics. During this merriment, up came an unsuspecting neighbor of the Hassans, Dick Ryan. He and Hassan were forced to fight each other for the gang's amusement.

When they had finally had all the happiness they could stand, they rode away, threatening that if the two men ever testified against the gang, "our friends will kill you."

How fearful everybody in the Hassan household must have been about what would come next, but the gang had had enough fun for one night and did not return. Terrified, Mrs. Hassan had hidden in a cornfield, for her husband had been gone so long that she thought the outlaws had carried out their threat to murder him. Hassan was picked up by a passing neighbor and returned to his home, exhausted but safe. A posse appeared but could not pick up the gang's tracks until the next morning.

By now word of their depredations had spread, and dozens of men were out searching for them, Indian, white, and black.

The Bucks were not through. Their next stop was Orcutt, where they invaded the local store and took their choice of the merchandise. The owner was gone, out with a posse hunting the Buck Gang, but he had had the foresight to take the store's cash along with him. His two young sons were minding the store. Fortunately, the gang paid no attention to the kids, but looted the store of food and ammunition.

They went on to rob a big Norbury and Company store at Arbekochee, and there they got a little cash and a large quantity of ammunition and weapons, and still more food.

One tale recounts the Bucks' robbery of a store in Okmulgee. Their next stop, said a citizen, would be Severs' store. Warned of the gang's approach, the story goes, the storekeeper at Severs' hastened to hide the cash, swollen to "something like $20,000 . . . as a payment had been made to the Indians and their accounts had been paid two or three days before." It was taken to the second floor of the building and stuffed into the pockets of some of the men's suits that hung there.

In the event, the gang did not appear at Severs', but they were not through with little businesses. This time it was a grocery store in the village of McDermott. They were looking for cash, but they found none and vented their anger and disappointment by smashing the store owner's display furniture and covering the floor with his sugar and flour.

They finished their day's entertainment by robbing still another store owner, a man named Knobble, leaving him tied up and poorer by a couple of sacks full of merchandise.

According to the reminiscences of a territorial old-timer, along the way the gang raped still another woman, a lady named Smith, whose farm was only some four miles from Rufus Buck's own home. On the trail of the gang, a lawman staked out the Buck place, but the outlaws did not return.

Nobody knows why the gang assumed they could carry on their reign of terror in the same general area of the Territory, repeated again and again. The answer may be as simple as this: They were simply too stupid or too arrogant to understand that you can't push people around forever without making them mad.

Which was what happened. Now on their trail were a host of hunters, including Captain Edmund Harry and other officers of the Creek Lighthorse police, plus two deputy U.S. marshals, heading a monstrous posse of angry citizens that may have numbered as many as a hundred men, both white and Indian. The outlaws' trail could not have been hard to find and follow, for by midday on August 10 the pursuers had found the Buck Gang at a place north of Okmulgee called Flat Rock.

The outlaws were sitting in a circle in the shade of a grove of trees below a knoll about two hundred feet high and about a quarter acre in extent. They were intent on splitting up a heap of loot taken in the store robberies and were squabbling over who got what. Buck finally tired of listening to the wrangling and told them that he was in charge and they'd get what he said they could have and nothing else. That fiat aroused considerable ill will, and they soon returned to fighting over the booty.

Once more the gang members demonstrated their intellectual poverty. Buck himself seems to have been particularly dense, for as the leader, he should have seen to having some sort of security. Any man with an IQ greater than eleven would have guessed that the law was hunting hard for them. Even so, they did not post a sentry on the high ground above them, from which an alert man could have spotted the posse before they closed in.

And so the wrangling over the loot continued, until, that is, the posse opened fire. Men on the trail of rapists in that faraway time understandably did not assign a high priority to due process of law, but somehow the first volley missed the outlaws. The gang could not reach their horses, however, and so they grabbed their weapons and scrambled to the top of the little hill. There they began to fire back at the posse.

The firing was heavy. One of the outlaws' rounds went through Captain Harry's hat, creasing his skull and knocking him off his horse. Once Harry had shaken off the shock of the bullet, he turned out to be unwounded and went back into the fight.

For a while the situation was a stalemate, for while the outlaws had the advantage of fighting from the high ground, they were heavily outnumbered by the men of the posse. Messengers galloped off to spread the news all the way to Fort Smith while the lawmen began to slowly crawl up the hill under a broiling sun.

At Fort Smith the first reports told of a "furious battle," even of fighting "hand to hand." Judge Parker, as usual imperturbable, carried on with his crowded docket while excitement in the streets of the town rose higher and higher. The courtroom was abuzz, too, and from time to time Judge Parker had to call for order. Crowds milled about in the streets of the town, waiting for news. What would happen, people asked, relieved that the lawmen had found and engaged these fiendish outlaws. Would any of the posse be hurt? Would the rapists sell their lives dearly? Could they possibly slip away?

Meanwhile, around the little knoll bullets flew back and forth for seven hours, without anybody on either side being hurt at all. But as the men of the posse inched up the slopes of the hill, they knew that in the end they had only to wait, for they could resupply with ammunition and the Bucks could not. But they kept on, and sooner or later posse members could work far enough up the sides of the little hill that they could rush the gang at close range.

Meanwhile, Marshal S. Martin Rutherford was hurrying from Muskogee with another posse, arriving about sundown to see the coming evening flickering with the flash of muzzle blasts and a pall of smoke hanging over the hilltop and the terrain around it. Rutherford seems to have closed up his posse to reinforce the men on the reverse slope of the hill, insuring that nobody was going to escape that way.

As night began to fall, the lawmen worked in closer and closer, shooting at muzzle flashes in the gathering darkness. The fire was still intense, and about then an old Euchee Indian posseman named Shansey got tired of lying on his belly exchanging fire with the Bucks on top of their rise as the lawmen inched up the hill.

He said something about standing to fight like a man, and then rose to his feet and fired a "dynamite cartridge" at the hilltop, a rifle round with a bit of explosive jammed into a hole in the tip of the bullet. It is a little hard to understand why such a round would not go off in the rifle, whose barrel and action were never designed for explosions heavier than the powder charge in the cartridge.

Nevertheless, according to legend, this round exploded against a tree on the bandits' hill, and a fragment cut through Rufus Buck's cartridge belt. Buck abruptly lost all his arrogance and courage and all interest in continuing the battle. He was petrified, threw down his rifle, and turned away to flee. His companions panicked, too, and the whole gang took to their heels over the rear of the rise, straight into the arms of Rutherford's men. The hoodlums had had enough and did not try to resist. So much for the bold revolutionaries.

Buck, Maomi July, and Lucky Davis were immediately appre-hended. Both Lewis Davis—who had a bullet hole in one leg—and Sampson managed to hide from the posse and remained free. It would not be for long.

In another account of the fight on the hilltop, the outlaws had simply run out of ammunition and surrendered. In any case they were not boastful now, and for all their posturing and big talk, not a one of them had chosen to go out in a blaze of glory like Ned Christie or Bill Doolin. Their brief careers had ended with a whimper.

The prisoners were loaded with chains and taken into tiny McDermott, where relieved Creek people appeared from all direc-tions to see the unspeakable scum who had murdered and raped and terrified decent people. Marshal Rutherford of the Northern District was in command now, and he was understandably worried about the continued existence of his prisoners. Crowds had gath-ered in the streets, and there was a great deal of murmuring about lynching.

Rutherford went out to speak to the crowd and promised that the outlaws would be taken to Fort Smith and tried in Judge Parker's dreaded court. There would be justice, he said, and reminded the town that he was duty-bound to defend the prisoners. He would do it, he told them, and "my men will shoot straight. The life of one of you is not worth the lives of all of them."

For a while things quieted down, but then men began to remember federal criticisms about Creek indifference to law enforcement in the nation, and once again the temper of the town turned sour. The mob began to post guards to make sure the mar-shals and their charges did not slip away in the darkness.

Rutherford could see what was coming, and he knew he had to get his prisoners out of town to avoid a lynching or a firefight or both. Now, said the marshal to the prisoners, you have a chance to save your own lives. We are going to try to escape this mob, but we can't have your chains clanking in the gloom. If we do, you will probably die on the nearest tree right here in town. So pick up your chains and carry them, he said, and keep them from rattling if you value your lives at all. They did, and for about half a mile lawmen and prisoners moved stealthily away from the murmuring mob.

Rutherford's caution paid off, for in the darkness he got his charges to Muskogee without incident, and then onto a train to Fort Smith. They would live a little longer.

In Fort Smith the gang was led down Garrison Avenue to the government barracks enclosure and then across it to the jail. It being a Sunday morning, "church bells tolled a requiem to the dead victims," according to one colorful account of the time. There the gang disappeared into cells to await trial, while the lawyers for both sides prepared their cases and witnesses were called to Fort Smith. The grand jury returned a true bill on the indictment of the gang for the rape of Rosetta Hassan, and on August 20 the gang members were arraigned before Judge Parker.

After the fight at the hilltop, Lewis Davis had gotten clear and reached the home of the Richardson family, where he hoped to hide. It was not long, however, before his leg wound began to go bad, apparently from blood poisoning. Mr. Richardson got word out to the law, and officers converged on the Richardson place. They did not have long to wait. Davis came out of the house, carrying his rifle, and started washing his wound. But when he straightened up and reached for his weapon, it was gone.

Richardson had taken the rifle, and the law moved in and led Davis away down the road to Fort Smith. There he joined the rest of the gang behind bars and doctors treated his wound, which turned out to be minor. Along with Buck and Lucky Davis, he was indicted for the Garrett murder, and he joined all of the gang under indictment for the attempted murder of Sam Houston and rape of Mrs. Hassan.

At trial Assistant U.S. Attorney J.B. McDonough had plenty of ammunition. He led off with Hassan and Ryan, whose testimony was damning enough. But then Mrs. Hassan took the stand.

The courtroom was dead silent while Mrs. Hassan testified, crying as she did so. There was, a reporter wrote, "scarcely a dry eye" in the jury box, and women in the courtroom cried in sympathy for the lady on the stand. Even the tough Judge Parker was seen to wipe his eyes.

Mrs. Hassan left the stand without cross-examination, the lawyers "standing aside and bowing reverently" as she passed. After that there was no doubt of the verdict. When it came time for final arguments, one of the appointed defense counsel simply announced to the jury and Judge Parker: "May it please the court and you gentlemen of the jury, I have nothing to say." There wasn't much else he could say.

Prosecutor McDonough passed up argument as well, simply telling the jurors that they had heard the evidence and he would expect a conviction. He got it as to all five of the gang. It took three minutes. It is said that the jury did not even sit down to deliberate.

Parker then excused that jury and seated a new one. This time the charge was the murder of Marshal Garrett, of which Rufus Buck and the two Davises stood accused. Buck tried to offer an alibi, saying he wasn't there; he was someplace else "after recruits" for his gang. The jury wasn't having any of the alibi, and this time it returned in just twelve minutes with a verdict of guilty as to all three men.

Judge Parker delayed sentencing for two more days, and then the gang faced the tall, stern judge. Parker addressed Rufus Buck's case first, adding to the legal language a lecture for the soul of the gang's leader, something he often did when announcing sentence:

> The verdict is an entirely just one, and one that must be
> approved by all lovers of virtue. . . . The Lawmakers of the
> United States have deemed your offense equal in enor-
> mity and wickedness to murder. It has been proven beyond
> question.

And then, to nobody's surprise, devout Judge Parker sentenced Buck to hang and added,

> May God, whose laws you have broken, and before whose
> tribunal you must appear, have mercy on your soul.

The other outlaws got the same sentence. They were first asked whether they had anything to say, as was the custom. Only Lucky Davis responded. "Yes," he said, "I want my case to go up to the Supreme Court." "I don't blame you," said the judge, and went on with his long and forbidding sentencing speech.

> This horrible crime now rests upon your souls. Remove it if you can so the good God of all will extend you His forgiveness and His mercy.

Execution was delayed while Buck's lawyer lodged an appeal with the U.S. Supreme Court, which under a curious jurisdictional quirk was the direct appellate authority over the Western District of Arkansas. Buck's claim on appeal was again that he could have produced evidence giving himself an alibi had he been allowed additional time to prepare for trial. The Supreme Court was not impressed, and all that remained was the hanging.

Buck created a curious document while he was awaiting execution. He had found religion, apparently, or pretended he did. In a letter to his wife, he enclosed a bit of crude poetry, full of misspellings and scribbled on the back of a picture of his mother. It included a rough drawing of a cross planted firmly in the Rock of Ages. On the cross he printed "Holy Ghost, Father, Son" and down below it "Virtue and Resurrection" and "Remember Me."

The *Muskogee Phoenix* called the drawing "really clever," a considerable exaggeration, and announced, "It makes a splendid photograph, and for those who wish curious mementoes of outlaws and other people, will no doubt be much sought after."

And so, on July 1, 1896, the Buck Gang was led out to the monstrous six-rope gibbet, said to be the largest in the United States, and there they were put down on a bench to reflect on what was about to happen next. A priest who had ministered to the defendants in jail said a prayer, and Rufus Buck's father tried to climb up to the gibbet platform. He was stumbling drunk, however, and lawmen barred his way.

Marshal George Crump formally read the death warrants. Then he turned to the gang members and asked, as was the custom of the time, whether any of them had any last words. A couple of them called out to people in the audience, but otherwise they were silent. Except for Lewis Davis, that is, who made the curious request that he be hanged alone. No, said the marshal, and all that was left to do was get on with the execution.

And when the trap dropped, the good people of eastern Indian Territory breathed a lot easier and slept better at night. The *Fort Smith Elevator* reported the demise of the gang under a brief and descriptive headline.

"Five Strung Up," it read. And it was so.

Chapter 7

STAGECOACHES AND TRAINS

THE GREAT WESTERN COTTAGE industry of train and stagecoach robbing reached its zenith in the second half of the nineteenth century and the first decade of the twentieth. The railroad express cars were a prime target, for they often carried substantial amounts of money; that's how banks moved hard cash from place to place. There was registered mail, too, often a source of money in transit between businesses or families. Stagecoaches were an even better target and were hit far more often even than trains.

Rather than rob banks, or in addition to robbing them, some hard cases reasoned that it might be more efficient to cut out the middleman and harvest the cash before a bank could lock it up in the vault. Train and stagecoach robbery had a couple of distinct advantages over knocking over banks.

First, trains were open all night; so were coaches, sometimes. Banks weren't. Operating under cover of darkness was a big help if you wanted to remain uninterrupted and unknown. Second, when you stopped a stagecoach or a train at some isolated place, you normally had to contend only with the coach driver and sometimes a guard, or with the train crew and the express agent.

Banks, on the other hand, were always in a town, where you might run into a town lawman, or more than one, and a flock of armed citizens, who were not inclined to mercy toward people who invaded their beloved city. Getting into town was easy; getting out again presented a myriad of problems. Then, even if you could get away, there was the telegraph, which could alert other lawmen to cut off your escape.

And so train and stagecoach robbery became the employment of choice for a goodly number of hoodlums in the years after the Civil War. The train robbers ranged all the way from the really dangerous Dalton Gang to buffoons like inept, posturing Al Jennings and stupid, drunken Elmer McCurdy. Elmer and Al have a place in this book, but it's in "Disorganized Labor" (the next chapter), for Al and Elmer were oafs, in spades.

Wells Fargo kept pretty fair records. In the fourteen years between 1870 and 1884, they show an astonishing 313 robberies or attempted robberies of stages, reaching a total of almost 500 by the turn of the century. And that doesn't count robberies of other stage lines not carrying Wells Fargo expresses.

The company's records also reflect the casualties: Four stage drivers and two guards were killed, and ten more were badly wounded. Four passengers were killed and two wounded.

Then there were the bandits. Five of them were killed during actual robberies, eleven more perished when the law caught up with them, and seven departed this earth at the hands of "citizens," as the company's report chastely put it. There would be more deaths in later years, although the days of the stagecoach were numbered.

Train robbery added to the toll. The first recorded robbery occurred in 1870, and from that time to century's end, in rough figures, there were some ninety attempts against trains, sixty-five of which succeeded. Counting the damage done during the stagecoach holdups, the grand total reached eighty-one outlaws killed in the act or hanged later. Eighteen lawmen died, along with fourteen possemen, six passengers, and twenty-one train crew.

That the toll wasn't worse was the work of many law enforcement agencies, guards, drivers, and ordinary citizens who fought back, and of Wells Fargo's own agents. The most successful was probably big Bob Paul, a quiet, gentle man who rose to be sheriff of Pima County, Arizona, to special officer of the Southern Pacific Railroad, to U.S. marshal of Arizona Territory. Wyatt Earp called him "as fearless a man and as fast a friend as I ever knew."

A lot of otherwise honest people considered train robbery to be something less than a mortal sin, since railroads were not loved overmuch by most small farmers. The railroad magnates controlled an enormous amount of land on both sides of the right-of-way, and farmers often felt—rightly or wrongly—that the railways charged exorbitant rates to ship to market the product of the farmers' sweat, that produce on which their livelihood depended.

On the other hand, if you had to spend any time looking down the barrel of a gun or watching a robber make off with the gold watch that had been your father's, you did not confuse these thugs with Robin Hood. This was especially so if you were an express agent—brave men, those—sitting inside an express car while bandits threatened to blow you and the car to kingdom come with dynamite.

For these felons didn't hesitate to brutalize express agents to get into the express safes, in which the really valuable loot was locked. And if the agent was true to his salt, as a lot of them were, if he forted up in the express car and made a fight of it, he ran a very real chance of having the car blown up and himself killed or maimed.

The railroads quickly went to the system of "way safes" and "through safes" in an effort to thwart repeated robberies. The express agent could get into the way safe, which contained comparatively small amounts of money for little towns along the right-of-way. The through safe protected the real money, gold or currency, and it was destined to go all the way through to the train's final or first major destination. Only there could it be opened by station personnel. This safe the express agent on the train could not open, having no keys.

On occasion train-robbing gangs were able to blast open a through safe, but that evolution took real talent, something most outlaws were markedly short of. There are even cases in which bumbling train robbers managed to destroy the entire express car, leaving the stout iron safe untouched—and still locked.

There were steady casualties among train crews, ranging from conductors shot down as they tried to drive off attackers to engineers and firemen crushed or scalded to death in the wreckage of their locomotives when robbers pried away a couple of fishplates and tore loose a rail.

Passengers were regularly robbed of whatever jewelry they wore and what cash they might have in their pockets. Train robbers often went through the cars demanding the passengers' valuables, usually after they had seen what the express car had to offer. One particularly small-souled group of robbers even included the train crewmen's lunches with their other loot.

But the railroad men and the passengers often got some of their own back, sometimes with the help of lawmen, sometimes entirely on their own. This chapter is mostly about some of those courageous folks and the toll they took of the train-robbing brotherhood in the years after the Civil War.

There was, for example, the saga of a couple of members of the vaunted Wild Bunch, who decided to stick up the Southern Pacific line. It happened at Sanderson, Texas, on March 13, 1912, when Ben Kilpatrick (the Tall Texan) and Ole Beck or Hobeck (also called Ed Welsh) decided it would be a fine idea to fatten their wallets by robbing a train.

Just the year before Ben had finished ten years in prison for train robbery. You'd think he would have learned from his long sojourn behind bars, but maybe that enforced vacation had only sharpened his appetite for express cars. As we shall see, Ben could easily have a place in the "Disorganized Labor" chapter. He certainly qualifies as an oaf.

But on this occasion, things went well at first. The chief express messenger, David Troutsdale (sometimes Trousdale), showed no signs of putting up a fight, as so many of his compatriots did. His apparent submission—and that of his two helpers—must have

Ben Kilpatrick, and Ole Beck, after being killed
near Sanderson, Texas, 1912, in attempt to hold

Extinct holdup men: Beck and Fitzpatrick.

OKLAHOMA UNIVERSITY WESTERN HISTORY LIBRARY

pleased these two experienced outlaws: an easy payday, no trouble, no shooting, no spilled blood, no noise.

No fuss at all, just money.

Troutsdale continued to be an agreeable, pacific sort. While Beck was outside the express car watching the train crew, Troutsdale stood with equanimity the arrogant Kilpatrick's bullying, which included a series of painful blows from the outlaw's Winchester.

"Get a move on," said the bandit, and Troutsdale did; the agent's action was not, however, exactly what Kilpatrick had in mind. "This is the most valuable parcel in the car," said Troutsdale helpfully, indicating a package with the toe of his shoe. Intrigued, the outlaw bent down to retrieve the prize.

At this Troutsdale picked up an ice maul, a heavy wooden mallet designed to crush big chunks of ice into smaller pieces to keep cool the succulent oysters so beloved in the early West. The maul was lying conveniently to hand on top of a nearby barrel of oysters, and with this handy implement the express agent bashed Kilpatrick in the back of the head.

He then hit the bandit twice more for good measure, distributing such brains as he had here and there about the express car. Having put an instant end to Kilpatrick, the doughty Troutsdale prepared for further action.

The dead bandit had been armed to the teeth: a Winchester and not one, but two, revolvers shoved into his belt. Troutsdale kept the Winchester for himself and handed a pistol each to his two helpers, men named Reagan and Banks. And then, wisely, the three agents waited for a while to see what else might befall. Nothing did. And so, unwilling to wait for further developments, Troutsdale fired a shot through the roof of the car. That got almost immediate results.

A voice was heard, a voice that called out for "Frank." The messenger could not be sure, but he assumed—quite correctly, as it turned out—that the voice surely had to belong to Beck. Peering around a pile of baggage, Troutsdale saw the outline of a head, somebody lurking behind the stacks of trunks and valises and boxes. He soon got a clear view of the lurker behind the baggage and drove a rifle bullet through Ole Beck, creating a quaint third eye just above the robber's real one on the left side of his head.

So much for the tough gun of the famous Wild Bunch and his dense companion.

The robbers who stopped a Rock Island train at Pond Creek, southbound from Wichita in 1894, had similar problems. There were at least four of them. (One account includes in the gang Charlie Pitts of James-Younger Gang fame, but that would have been something of a miracle since Charlie had been quite dead since the Northfield raid back in 1876.) Whoever the outlaws were, they stopped the train all right, but then the operation came unraveled in a hurry.

When their demands to open the express car were ignored by express agent John Crossland, they detonated a stick of dynamite under the door. Stunned, Crossland played for time while guard Jake Harmon slipped out the back door of the car, moved through another car, and stepped quietly out into the night.

Seeing a pack of bandits outside the express car, including one who was brandishing a pistol, Harmon gave the pistol waver a dose of buckshot. The outlaw went down, and general panic and consternation followed. The rest of the bandits ran off into the gloom. One was captured immediately; two more were run down later and jailed.

As another bunch of train robbers discovered the hard way, it didn't pay to fool with agent Jeff Milton, later a legendary Arizona lawman. The gang found out one day at Southern Pacific's Fairbank station, down in Cochise County, Arizona. As the train stood in the station and Milton handed down packages from the express car, somebody in a crowd of bystanders ordered, "Throw up your hands and come out of there."

Milton's answer was not what the voice wanted to hear: "If there's anything in here you want, come and get it!" The answer was a bullet that knocked off Milton's hat; more bullets smashed into his left arm and knocked him down.

Milton was not about to quit. He had his shotgun, but he coolly held his fire, worried about hitting some innocent civilian if he simply sprayed buckshot at the robbers. In the event, the outlaws solved his problem. Apparently sure Milton was dead or too badly hurt to resist, the outlaws now started to climb through the express car door.

So it came as a nasty surprise when Milton, shooting one-handed, opened fire with his shotgun at the first bandits to enter the car. The first outlaw through the door was Three-Fingered Jack Dunlap, who promptly expired of eleven pieces of buckshot. A single buckshot wounded Bravo Juan Yoas; embarrassingly, he was hit in the fanny, presumably as he turned tail to run. Yoas lost all interest in further larceny.

The other three bandits poured bullets into the express car, but by this time Milton had lost consciousness, sheltered on the floor between two trunks. The surviving bandits could now enter the car. But the safe was locked and they could not get it open. They had no dynamite—gosh, I knew we'd forgotten something—and they could not find the safe keys. Milton had thoughtfully thrown them away before he lost consciousness.

In the fall of 1894, a gang demonstrated a tried-and-true means of stopping your prey. They chose an Atchison, Topeka and Santa Fe train, and their system worked. Easy: You wave a red lantern as if you were the station agent, and the train stops. The bandits badly wounded the engineer and then went on to the express car to find the rich shipment they thought was there.

But it wasn't. Instead, the car contained a band of tough Santa Fe detectives, who had been tipped off about the robbery. The leader of the outlaw gang went down dead, full of holes, and a second bandit managed to get clear but was soon captured. Two other bandits got away clean, which tells you something about the detectives' shooting.

March 27, 1895, was an even better night for the law. Train number 3 of the Cincinnati Southern Railway was stopped by a lantern-waving figure in a deep cut just north of Greenwood,

Kentucky. Four bandits emerged from the gloom, all obviously rank amateurs at train robbing. They headed straight for the baggage car, apparently thinking it was the express car. As they busily ransacked the wrong car, back in a passenger car three railroad detectives got suspicious and walked forward to find out what the trouble was.

The first detective was confronted by a bandit who gave the usual "Hands up" order, but the cop went for his pistol instead, and in the close-range fight that followed the outlaws came in a bad second. One took a bullet in the heart, which saw him off immediately. A second badman survived only two hours, shot through the lungs. Still a third was so badly shot up that he almost died.

The presence of the three detectives on the train was no accident, for they had been warned about the robbery. The informer had ridden along on the raid, but wisely elected to hold the outlaws' horses and stay out of the line of fire.

Railroad detectives ranked right up there as the outlaws' worst enemies, and one of the most deadly of them was a quiet, retiring man called Fred Hans. In 1900 he worked for the Northwestern Railroad, which in those days ran between Deadwood and Omaha, often hauling very large shipments of gold from the Deadwood mines. He was very good at his job, so good outlaws mostly steered well clear of the Northwestern.

He was so tenacious that a band of outlaws he had been chasing tried to ambush him. They killed his horse, but Hans dropped behind the animal's carcass and opened fire. He was deadly with his two pistols, putting a round through one ambusher's heart and killing another man's horse. He drilled another bullet through a third bandit's brain and shot a fourth in the belly. The remaining bandit wisely quit.

In 1896 the storied Christian brothers gang—called the High Fives after a card game popular at the time—tried for a bonanza at Rio Puerco trestle, a small station on the Atlantic and Pacific Railroad, thirty-plus miles from Albuquerque. There on an October evening A&P train number 2 contracted a mechanical hiccup and pulled to a stop near the station.

The problem was quickly fixed, but as the train started up again, two outlaws swung on board and fired at a brakeman on the station platform, wounding him in the hand, an act both wholly unnecessary and very stupid indeed. The engineer pulled the train to a halt.

Now there had been no reason to shoot at the brakeman, but the shot did warn Kohler, the express messenger, who put out the lights, locked the express car door, and readied his revolver. Back in a passenger car, Deputy U.S. Marshal Will Loomis, also alerted by the ill-advised shot, picked up his shotgun and stepped outside to investigate.

As the bandits approached the express car door, the express messenger let drive through the door of the car, and Loomis walked through the darkness toward the head of the train. He waited until one man, obviously an outlaw, stepped away from a knot of men gathered around the express car door and then took his shot.

His buckshot knocked down the bandit, one Cole (or Code) Young, but Young managed to pull himself to his feet and fire two wild shots at Loomis, or at the flash of his shotgun. Loomis fired the other barrel and Young fell permanently, rolling down the embankment in the darkness.

The outlaws dithered a while—there was that pesky express agent still shooting at them through the car door—and finally, apparently still unaware that Young was dead, rode off into the night, empty-handed after a thoroughly inept performance.

This failure simply confirmed that it didn't take much to be a famous outlaw—the High Fives were already the authors of a preposterously inept performance in an attempted robbery in Juarez, Arizona; that farce qualified them for some space in the chapter called "Disorganized Labor."

If the railroads had a tough row to hoe, the problem for the stage lines was worse. It was easy enough to choose a spot in the middle of nowhere, where the coach had to slow down to a walk and there was good cover for the criminal. At a place like that any stagecoach was cold meat, even one driven by a "*jehu*," frontier slang for a driver who pushed his horses to frightening speeds.

Some turns were so sharp, some grades so steep, that even a *jehu* had to slow down. Even rank amateurs like Joe Boot and Pearl Hart—who appear elsewhere—could manage at least one successful stage robbery if they gave just a little thought to it.

But there were hazards.

Stagecoach passengers and guards tended to be abrupt and irritable when highwaymen tried to interrupt their peaceful progress from place to place. It was bad enough eating dust and rattling around in a swaying coach without people stealing your hard-earned money and precious possessions.

Still, the stage driver, no matter how competent, had his work cut out for him. Take, for example, the roads—such as they were—in and out of Bodie, California, and Virginia City, Nevada. To paraphrase William Tecumseh Sherman's comment about Texas, any sensible person who inherited both Hell and Bodie would live in Hell and rent out Bodie.

For these mining towns were as tough and dangerous places as the West ever produced, and that includes Tombstone, Deadwood, and the Kansas cow towns like Abilene, Newton, and Dodge. The book *U.S. West: The Saga of Wells Fargo*, talking about Bodie, put it perfectly:

> The local shootings, bludgeonings, stabbings, hackings, horsewhippings, gougings and more casual mayhem vied in the fine agate print of the *Bodie Free Press* with almost daily accounts of larceny on a grand scale and assaults of frightening frequency upon tangible property of every sort.

At one point in 1879, a visitor recalled that in his first week in town Bodie produced six fatal shootings.

In those wild and woolly days, the "bad man from Bodie" was a commonplace handle for virtually any loud, nasty bully anyplace in the West, especially California. If the term was a half-humorous generality elsewhere, out on the stage routes in and out of Bodie the reference was deadly serious.

For while they lasted, Bodie's mines produced a king's ransom in treasure, and such a tempting chance for instant wealth drew professional and amateur badmen like flies to bad meat, waiting out on the lonely roads the stagecoaches had to travel to haul all these riches out of Bodie.

The coach crews had to be tough and courageous, and in the eyes of some perhaps a little crazy. But they were equal to the challenge, repeatedly fighting off or racing through attempted holdups.

Similar hazards were common on the roads in and out of Virginia City, a similar boom town. One of the stage drivers who confronted the dangers of that run was a very tough man who rejoiced in the handle of Shotgun Bill Taylor. According to the abiding legend of Taylor, he got almighty tired of being held up. Accordingly, he rigged up a shotgun—presumably a sawed-off double-barrel—so that it would fit up the right leg of his trousers. With an ingenious arrangement of wires, he was able to fire it by a simple pull of his fingers.

As the story goes, when a road agent appeared to demand that Taylor halt his coach and stand and deliver his valuable cargo, Taylor obligingly raised his right foot to push down on the coach brake, a wooden spar sticking up from the front wheels.

And when his right leg was appropriately aligned, Taylor twitched his wire and the unsuspecting bandit got the full benefit of an eight- or ten-gauge load of buckshot: very little due process, that, but very efficient indeed. It is not recorded what Shotgun Bill did when the bandit approached from some other direction.

Nobody knows how many eager, greedy bandits Shotgun Bill erased over the years—he and Wells Fargo were the only ones who kept score. But whatever the finally tally was, Wells Fargo was surely grateful, so much so that at the 1893 world's fair in Chicago the company's exhibit included a statue of Taylor—with his right foot raised.

Stagecoach robbery in America is said to have gotten its start in California, of all places, with a gang put together by Tom Bell—not his real name—a plug-ugly brawler who sported a nose squished almost flat on his face in some long-ago fight. Although Dick Turpin, the dashing English highwayman, had pioneered the gentle art of stage robbery a century before, this business of stopping a stage en route to rob it was something new to the United States.

Bell's gang dates from about 1854, when he put together a coven of ex-cons: Juan Fernandez, English Bob, Monte Jack, Jim Smith, and one Convery, also called Connor. Most of these names were obviously aliases, and the gang was as motley as its names.

Other hoodlums drifted in and out of the gang from time to time. Perhaps because of this bewildering, ever-changing collection of criminals, or maybe from a love of the dramatic, Bell is said to have devised a secret sign—a bullet hung on a string—which you dangled about to announce yourself to other gang members. Nothing very obvious about that . . .

The gang had its chance at a really big strike in August 1856, when a spy told them that the stage to Marysville was carrying gold dust, as much as one hundred thousand dollars' worth, an enormous sum for the day. Bell had a plan that even might have worked. He intended to flank the road with three men on each side and produce a cross fire, but one trio got lost in thick brush and were AWOL when the coach appeared. And so, when the stage passed, there was only one group of thugs in proper position.

The guard, a tough cookie named Dobson, didn't hesitate. He blazed away, and so did some armed passengers. The driver didn't hesitate either, and before the outlaws could recover, their prize was gone, galloping off down the road.

The bandits had taken no serious casualties, but several passengers on the stage were hurt, none seriously but one: Tragically, the wife of the town barber in Marysville had been killed. The temper of the town's citizens turned very ugly, and the hunt was on.

A posse jumped a tent full of the gang members and gave them a chance to surrender. "No, never!" shouted one, and reached for his pistol. He shouldn't have, for those were the last words he ever spoke. Four others with him thought better of resistance and went off to jail. Five more outlaws went into the bag soon after, and another clash netted Convery, quite dead.

Gristy, another gang member, was captured when a man who knew him in his prison days turned him in. And Gristy immediately lost all semblance of loyalty and told lawmen where Bell's hideout was; Bell was also captured soon afterward. The sheriff was sent for, but before he arrived, the posse remembered the barber's wife. All the due process Bell got was, as westerners used to say, a big, tall tree and a short piece of rope.

But Bell had started something that became almost an art form in the western states. It produced countless legends and myriad bad movies, and it was even responsible for the production of the first real armored vehicle, called the Monitor, presumably named for the Civil War Union ironclad.

It was an armored stagecoach, complete with firing ports, and it appeared on a much-robbed line in Wyoming, with one terminus at wild Deadwood. Generally staffed by three armed guards, it carried large shipments of treasure between Deadwood and Cheyenne, sometimes as much as one hundred thousand dollars' worth; at least one shipment was worth a cool quarter of a million.

And the armored coach worked well for a while, until a group of bandits smarter than the usual ambushed it at a small way station. A wild battle ensued, in which one passenger was killed, one guard wounded, and one bandit badly shot up.

The inevitable pursuit by a posse was relentless. At least two outlaws were run down and hanged out of hand. The lawmen who came upon the scene later simply left them hanging, presumably for the edification of other would-be criminals. As the French say, *pour encourager les autres.*

Another bandit fell into the hands of the law when a passerby recognized a gold bar from the shipment, now innocently displayed in a store window, and still another was pinched when he tried to sell jewelry stolen from the stage. Another bandit marginally involved, career criminal George "Big Nose" Parrott, escaped arrest but went right back to his evil ways.

Forming his own gang, he decided to hit a train near Carbon, Nebraska, and he did it in the cruelest possible way. He and his thugs pried loose a couple of fishplates and spread the rails, insuring that the train would derail and tumble down the embankment. It took them a couple of tries: The eastbound train that was their target roared through before they could finish their job.

But they persevered and managed to loosen a rail in time for the westbound train. This time, however, they reckoned without a railroad maintenance crew, moving down the railway on their handcar. The crew repaired the break and then pumped off to report the event. Big Nose George and his minions left empty-handed.

Curses! Foiled again!

And that wasn't all. Two lawmen followed them. The officers stopped at a fire George's boys had lit and found the ashes still warm. One lawman commented to the other that their quarry must be close, and the outlaws, near enough to hear them, opened fire. The killings just about ensured a bad end to their story.

Sure enough, when a gang member called Dutch Charley was run down by the law and shipped back for trial, a band of citizens intercepted the train carrying him, rooted him out of hiding in the baggage car, attached the necessary rope, and stood him on a barrel. The coup de grâce was a swift kick to the barrel, administered, with some justice, by the sister-in-law of one of the murdered lawmen.

Another gang member struck out on his own and lasted only a month before he was shot down during a botched attempt to rob the Black Hills stagecoach line.

Big Nose, meanwhile, had fled to the Powder River country in Montana. He might have stayed out of trouble and lived happily ever after, except that he suffered from an advanced case of criminal's disease: He couldn't keep his mouth shut. So—with the assistance of more booze than he could hold—he told everybody within earshot about what a bold, bad outlaw he was. His stupid antics got him arrested and sent south for trial—but Carbon was a stop on the way to Rawlins, where the court sat, and in Carbon a reception committee was waiting for the train.

Big Nose managed to avoid his final extinction at the Carbon depot—he said he'd give the law information if the mob let him live. They did, and he was moved on to Rawlins. In some haste he tried to plead guilty, but the judge wasn't sure of his mental condition and sent him back to his cell. And then His Honor turned to his clerk:

> Mr. Meldrum, I want you to go to the jail and interview
> the gentleman with the pronounced proboscis and ascertain
> whether he is compos mentis.

A week later, observed and advised, Big Nose returned to court and pleaded guilty. Not surprisingly, he was sentenced to death and returned to jail, his feet shackled, to await his date with the rope.

But Big Nose somehow got hold of a dining-table knife and carefully sawed away at his shackles. It took time, but he finally got loose and attacked the turnkey when the man brought in a meal, bashing the jailer in the skull with his shackles. He was out of his cell, but as he ran for the outside door, the jailer's wife hurried through it, locked it behind her, and produced a pistol. She told George he was a dead man if he went any farther. The outlaw believed her.

That was enough for the citizenry to act on their own. Big Nose died by the rope after all, a messy affair involving a broken rope and other ugly happenings. It was tough way to go.

A Dr. Osborne pronounced the obvious, that Big Nose was dead, and seeing an opportunity, he partially skinned the remains and, as a neat ballad later related,

> An' took some hide from off his chest,
> An' had it cured and tanned;
> An' made into a pair of shoes,
> That always used to stand,
> Right in his office window.

Or maybe, as another version tells us, the good doctor wore those shoes regularly; when he was elected the first Democratic governor of Wyoming, he wore that grim footwear to the inaugural ball. Notions of high style were a little different in those far-off days.

Hippocrates probably would not have approved, but the good doctor achieved a peculiar sort of lasting fame both for himself and Big Nose George. The shoes still exist.

The wife of the jailer who had acted in time to prevent escape was given a gold watch. Big Nose George himself followed in the footsteps of a good many other bandits and entered upon a second career. His remains spent the next year pickled in a whiskey barrel while medical experimentation continued, part of it an attempt to find some organic cause of his criminal ways. At the end of it he was buried, barrel and all.

In a sort of wry postscript, a newspaper commented that the warrant for Big Nose George had not been executed, "because on the day appointed for execution George Parrott could not be found in Carbon County."

A similar fate—minus the tanning—befell two robbers who ambushed a stage near Riverside, Arizona, in August 1883. They had murdered the messenger in cold blood, and so nobody bothered much with legal niceties when they were caught. Two of their comrades in crime made the mistake of trying to fight legendary sheriff Bob Paul; both got a quick trip to Boot Hill as a reward.

Nobody knows for sure who the last stage robbers were, but that dubious honor may belong to a Nevada psychopath named Ben Kuhl for a murderous attack on a peaceful man driving a mail wagon, successor to the coach. It was a very cold day in 1916 when Kuhl jumped on the wagon as it passed and then rammed a revolver against the back of driver Fred Searcy's head. Kuhl pulled the trigger, got a misfire, and tried again. Searcy was dead instantly, killed in cold blood.

The attack had been carefully planned, for Kuhl then propped Searcy up on the seat and drove the wagon down the road, past a house and a freighter's camp, and to a thicket, where he could ransack the mail at his leisure. Though people saw the wagon pass, the snow was falling too heavily to see that Searcy was lifeless.

Kuhl had hoped to find a payroll, but there wasn't any. He ended up with about four thousand dollars, a pitiful price for a man's life, and a search party quickly found the wagon, with Searcy frozen stiff on the seat. He had obviously been murdered, and the law had a couple of reasonably good clues.

The first was a dog, of all things, a dog that had unaccountably attached itself to Kuhl in spite of Kuhl's indifference to the critter. The searchers recognized the track of the animal, since there were few dogs that size in the area. So they brought the dog back to the wagon, and sure enough, the animal went straight to the pile of snow where Kuhl had stashed the mailbags. Meanwhile, a coat was found under a nearby footbridge, and somebody in town identified it as belonging to Kuhl.

Kuhl was arrested, partially on the basis of the canine evidence and the coat and partly based on a bloody palm print on a discarded envelope that appeared to match his. A gun in his cabin was found to have one expended round still in it, too, and the case went to trial.

The deciding factor was the palm print. Forensics was still in its infancy, but some fingerprint evidence had been allowed, although not yet in Nevada. Nevertheless, the judge admitted the palm print and the jury came back with a first-degree murder verdict. They made no recommendation as to sentence, so the choice was up to Kuhl. Hanging or shooting; take your pick. Kuhl chose the firing squad, but his sentence was commuted to life just a week before his big day, after the governor was deluged by pleading letters from a flock of bleeding hearts.

Considering what Kuhl had done, it was a crying shame.

No history of train robbery would be complete without a mention of John Sontag and Christopher Evans, a pair of Californians. Greed, according to some sources, was not the primary motivation for their violent two-man crime wave, which left a good deal of blood in its wake.

It was revenge.

Both men nursed grudges against the Southern Pacific. Evans believed the railroad had cheated him out of his land. In this he was not alone; the SP was cordially detested by many small farmers for the same reason, and for what they perceived as exorbitant freight rates. Sontag had been a brakeman with the Southern Pacific; he had been injured on the job and blamed the railroad for it. What followed was a series of at least five holdups, the last one also involving Sontag's younger brother George.

They began early in 1889, setting a pattern that they varied from but little in the rest of their jobs. They got onto the train's tender at a station, and once the locomotive had picked up speed, they threw down on the engineer and fireman and forced the train to halt. Then, herding their prisoners ahead of them, they went back to the express car. "Throw down the box," one of them ordered, but the express agent was not receptive.

The robbers' next step was to dynamite the express car door, which not only got it open but stunned the agent. It was an easy score, until three men came forward from the passenger cars to see what the problem was; one of them was a deputy sheriff. Evans and Sontag shot two of them, wounding the lawman and killing a passenger.

Almost a year later they hit a train again. They didn't need dynamite this time, because the express agent handed over the loot without a fuss. Maybe he did it so easily because there was a measly five hundred dollars in the box. But in the process of the robbery, the two outlaws wantonly shot down and killed an inoffensive hobo, who'd been hitching a ride and ran away when the train stopped.

Over a year after their second holdup, they made it three in a row near a Central Valley town called Alila, but this time it didn't go as well. In fact, it didn't go at all. They succeeded in seriously wounding the fireman and the express agent but had to gallop off empty-handed.

Since nobody had identified the pair for a certainty, suspicion fell on the Dalton brothers, a couple of whom were in the area at the time. They were not involved—in that particular crime, at least—and a year or so later Evans and Sontag struck again. And once again they got nothing for their trouble, but they left a badly wounded railroad detective on the ground behind them.

The last holdup, with their usual lack of original thought, came about a year later at a small station. This time Sontag's brother George came along, waiting for the pair in a buggy—of all things—behind a station building. As crimes go, this one was a real disaster. This time nobody would open the safe, so out came the dynamite. The robbers proceeded to demonstrate their abysmal incompetence as explosives experts. Three straight charges of dynamite were needed to open the all-important safe.

There was lots of coin in the steel box, but most of it turned out to be Peruvian. And the law discovered that George Sontag had rented a buggy, saying something about "going hunting in the mountains" (in a buggy?). But the buggy was returned the next day, and George couldn't resist talking at length about the holdup, albeit from what he imagined would have been a passenger's point of view. When officers talked to him, he gave a suspicious account of the robbery, enough to arouse the lawmen's interest.

And so a detective called Will Smith and a deputy sheriff named Witty went out to talk to John Sontag. What they found were both outlaws, who fired on the officers, wounding both of them, Witty badly. The outlaws ran for it, but the sheriff reasoned that they might return for supplies, and he was right.

The sheriff and two deputies closed in on the house, only to find Evans and Sontag were already there. In the ensuing firefight one lawman went down dying. The officers had made the mistake of ordering both men to surrender.

A small lawmen's posse followed the fugitives and two officers moved in to check on a shadowy figure they saw entering a cabin. Both Evans and Sontag were there, and the robbers promptly opened fire, killing both lawmen. Another officer was wounded, and once again Evans and Sontag got away.

Their next victim was a former deputy sheriff named Black, who was callously shot down on the grounds that he was an "informant." And pursuit was difficult for the law: The outlaws were getting help from both of their families, and perhaps a few other people who hated the railroad worse than murderers. More lawmen took the field, and now there was a general understanding that with these two, it would be better to shoot first and challenge afterward.

The end of the trail for Evans and Sontag came at a place called Stone Corral, up in the Tulare County foothills above the town of Visalia. This time it was the law that occupied the only structure, taking a rest at the end of a long day of fruitless hunting. Unaware, Evans and Sontag walked up to the house, and a wild firefight ensued.

One lawman was wounded, but both outlaws were shot full of holes. The officers heard Sontag begging Evan to shoot him, but Sontag was too engrossed in firing on the officers to do his partner that favor.

When the shooting died away, the officers wisely waited through the night before they closed in at daybreak. Sontag was lying unconscious behind a haystack and was taken down to Visalia. Evans was gone. With remarkable endurance he had managed to stagger seven miles, but he was captured without a fight the next day.

Sontag died a few days later; Evans survived to be tried for murder, but escaped the night before he was to be sentenced, using a gun smuggled in to him by, of all people, his daughter. He did not stay free long, for the lawmen staked out his home, where lived his wife and seven children—maybe the only people he really cared about—and Evans walked into their trap. Surrounded by a large posse, he was given the chance to surrender and spare his family possible injury. He did the right thing, for once.

He got life and served fourteen years of his sentence. On his release he spent some time touring the state with a "Crime does not pay" lecture—shades of Frank James—and he died three years later. So, when all the killing and fleeing and hiding were over, at the end of the trail of blood, the Southern Pacific came out ahead after all.

Famous—or infamous—horse outlaw Bill Doolin, a charter member of the Dalton Gang, tried his hand at train robbery, too. He was part of the disastrous holdup at Adair, Oklahoma, in 1892, which left a local doctor dying and sealed the fate of the Dalton brothers.

And in May 1893 he and two other career robbers, Bittercreek Newcomb and Henry Starr, lay in wait for a train near Ponca City, Oklahoma. They were thwarted by the heroism and acting ability of a young brakeman, who smelled a rat, managed to get the train stopped short of the station, and went forward to investigate.

When he met the three thugs, he managed to convince them that the train was alerted to the holdup and was carrying—which was true—big trouble for the outlaws: "Heck Thomas and Charley Stockton," he said, "and both are loaded for bear."

Bittercreek mumbled some threats to veteran lawmen Stockton and Thomas but did nothing about it; nobody in his right mind wanted to tangle with either one, let alone both at once. The outlaws did move up the track toward the halted train, but the brakeman's glib deception had bought enough time for a detail of soldiers from the nearby Ponca Indian Agency to reach the station. When they challenged and opened fire, Doolin and his two buddies ran for it, empty-handed.

Doolin led another train attack the next year near Cimarron, Kansas, but ran into a posse led by a local Sheriff. While Doolin evaded capture, the lawmen got a bullet into him, a steel-jacketed round that broke one foot. The injury would plague him all the rest of his few days, until he came in second in a fight with another of the Guardsmen, Heck Thomas, in 1896.

The same lack of success followed a gang of holdup men at Pond Creek, Oklahoma, just the next year. At first success seemed certain. The outlaws got the train stopped as planned, held the train crew hostage, and rushed to find their bonanza in the express car. Just two hundred dollars for all that risk.

Which brings us to the all-time scum of the train robbery profession, and what was one of the last such robberies on record. The DeAutremont brothers, professional criminals by choice, stopped a Southern Pacific train as it slowed for a tunnel at a place called Siskiyou Station, just on the Oregon-California border.

When the express agent refused to open the car, the brothers used dynamite, a monstrous charge that blew out the entire front of the car. It burst into flame. The agent died in either the explosion or the fire, and the fire was too intense for the brothers to enter and steal whatever good things lay inside.

When a brakeman ran forward toward the locomotive, the bandits killed him, too, maybe just because his appearance startled them. Worst of all, they callously murdered both the engineer and the fireman—standing with his hands up—probably to avoid any chance of later identification.

The investigating officers found evidence in profusion: backpacks to carry off the loot, a pair of stained coveralls, and a pistol among other things. Now there was no CSI in those far-off days, no complex sophisticated tests to run down evildoers, but the law went to the best there was at the time, a professor at the University of California. The professor examined the available evidence and deduced the identity of one of the murderers.

He was a lumberjack, said the professor; the pitch stains on the overalls proved that. The stains were in such a place that he was left-handed, and Douglas fir needles in the pockets placed him in the Northwest. Best of all, crammed in a pocket of the overalls was a tiny piece of faded paper. In the lab the professor brought out the writing on it, and it proved to be a registered mail receipt for a letter from one of the brothers to another.

While the Post Office went to work running down addresses to go with the names, the revolver was traced by its serial number to the point of sale, and the hunters found there a signed receipt. Although the name on the paper was false, the handwriting belonged to one of the brothers. The express tag on the bag revealed the identity of the sender: sure enough, another brother.

It was a brilliant job of investigation, but it remained to find the brothers, and that took some three years. The law didn't quit and spread pictures of the brothers literally worldwide, in English and five other languages. All the publicity finally paid off. A soldier came in to say that one of the photos looked like a fellow soldier he knew in the Philippines as Price. Sure enough, it was one of the wanted men, and all the publicity produced a witness from Ohio who worked with both remaining brothers.

With all of the professor's evidence, the prosecution got a conviction on one of the brothers, but unaccountably the jury recommended life in prison rather than execution. The other two pleaded guilty, got the same sentence, and the DeAutremont boys disappeared from history—it was a shame they weren't executed, but at least society was rid of them.

Chapter 8

DISORGANIZED LABOR

The Oafs

IN ONE SENSE, all outlaws are losers. There is no such thing as living happily ever after, surrounded by piles of your ill-gotten loot. But some criminals are exceptional failures, committing the most astonishing blunders and stupidities, virtually handing themselves over to a prison cell or the graveyard or both in order. Even those who last a long while—the James-Younger Gang is a good example—in time do something unimaginably stupid, and that stupidity leads to the end of the road, usually abruptly.

There is considerable evidence that low intelligence and a depraved family life commonly had a lot to do with the robbers' choice of profession. Those unglamorous traits show up with some frequency in the family history of professional robbers and, for that matter, in the background of professional criminals of all kinds.

Every student in Psychology 1 has heard of the Jukes and the Kallikaks, made-up names for two families studied by eugenicists who found them to be major suppliers of prisons and psychiatric hospitals. Similar studies were made of other families: the Nams, the Zeros, the Happy Hickories, and the Sam Sixties (supposedly named for the IQ of the family's patriarch). These families also produced bumper crops of criminals, prostitutes, pimps, generally feebleminded folks, and a certifiable loony or two.

A good example was the Smiddy family. Ennis Fay Smiddy was born sometime between 1903 and 1906, and he had a flock of siblings, five of whom were brothers: Curtis, called Green; Fred; Gene; Sam Earl; and Lonnie, also known as Buford. Ennis was the pioneer criminal of the brood, arrested for forgery and sent to prison in Texas about 1926.

After escaping, he embarked on a series of small-time gas station robberies, and then graduated to murder, shooting two unsuspecting lawmen outside a small-town dance. One lawman, dying, said brother Green Smiddy shot him, and witnesses saw not only Green but Ennis and even father Sam near the dance.

The family tried to provide alibis, Sam and another son were questioned and released, and Green and Ennis finally got out of jail because nobody could place them in the car from which the fatal shots were fired. Green went free, but Ennis went back to Texas to finish out his sentence.

He was just getting started. Paroled in 1930, he went off with some other worthless thugs and together they held up their first bank; two of his hoodlums were quickly caught, but Ennis managed to remain at large, branching out into burglary before he was again pinched and sent to prison for a five-year term.

In 1932 his brother Green was killed trying to rob a bank. Learning nothing from Green's demise, Ennis went back to his evil ways. It was auto theft this time. He was getting a reputation with the law, for he spent some days in jail in Duncan, Oklahoma, charged with "investigation," apparently a euphemism for "We're sure he's committed some crime but we're not sure what."

Nothing came of this, and upon his release Ennis and some other crooks ran up a string of ten bank robberies between May and November of 1934. That string ran out at Christmas of 1934 when a federal posse found Ennis at his brother-in-law's house. There was no resistance: Ennis was far too debilitated from a monumental drunk the night before.

He was in deep trouble now, exposed to the death penalty, which could be imposed under new federal legislation nicknamed the "Dillinger Law"— named for then active dean of bank robbers, John Dillinger. After a guilty plea—maybe because of it—Ennis got a mere seventy-seven years and went off to Alcatraz, where he died of liver failure in 1941. Significantly, perhaps, the Alcatraz management listed his IQ as fifty-four.

Indeed, intelligence was not generally a notable asset of these lower-tier bank robbers, even those who were not actual Kallikaks. Take a punk called Snow, who was forced to run for it when his getaway driver couldn't get the car to start. On foot, he was easy game for the law, who found him cowering in a cotton patch on the edge of town. Plan ahead, bad man: Keep the motor running or steal a reliable car.

A case of intellectual vacuum also beset the ordinarily efficient George Birdwell, frequent accomplice of Choc "Pretty Boy" Floyd, or maybe George was just having a bad day. Floyd was a canny outlaw, and Birdwell seemed at least ordinarily bright throughout most of his career as a robber, but Birdwell pulled what has to rank among the all-time stupid stunts when he and two others tried to rob the bank in little Boley, Oklahoma, in 1932.

Now Boley was an all-black town, one of many in Oklahoma, and maybe Birdwell thought it would be a pushover. He tried to interest Choc in the venture, but Floyd wanted no part of it; he even warned Birdwell not to go near the town, but Birdwell decided success was assured.

He was wrong, dead wrong in fact. The citizens of Boley were proud of their town and prepared for trouble because of the rash of bank robberies plaguing Oklahoma—a couple of banks had been looted in towns within miles of Boley. And so the citizens had stockpiled arms at the Masonic Hall, and David Turner, president and owner of the bank, had installed an alarm system.

Turner was a respected community leader, deeply concerned for the future of his town. He organized the downtown merchants, and the new burglar alarm sounded like the Last Trumpet inside the bank; it also rang in several nearby businesses.

It was Saturday and the streets were crowded. And it was the start of the prairie chicken season, and lots of people were buying shotgun ammunition. Not at all a good time to rob a bank. And to compound their lack of coherent planning, Birdwell and his two thugs parked their getaway car in front of the bank, pointing the wrong way, a casual oversight that left only one door instead of two to climb into in case of a hasty retreat.

Worse, it required a U-turn in order to turn back toward the highway and safety. The driver stayed with the car, and George and a helper walked into the bank and confronted Turner, who was working one of the teller's windows.

Looking down the muzzle of Birdwell's .45, Turner counted out bills until the removal of the last one automatically fired the alarm. "You pulled that alarm," snarled Birdwell. "I'll kill you for that!" The gutty bank president looked the bad man in the eye and said, "You bet I did," at which Birdwell shot Turner point-blank four times. As Turner fell dying, a teller, who had seen the trouble developing and crawled back to the vault out of sight below desk level, got the rifle stashed there, and now he put an abrupt end to Birdwell with a single round.

Birdwell's accomplice, Champ Patterson, and the getaway driver—who had heard the firing and run inside—took to their heels, forcing hostages to drag Birdwell's carcass out toward the car. At the same time the outlaws scrambled to scoop up stray bills from the floor where Birdwell had dropped them. They didn't get far. A citizen with a shotgun opened up on them as they left the bank, and at this happy distraction the hostages took flight.

Patterson went down hard just outside the door, riddled with several loads of birdshot, by one estimate as many as 450 of them. The driver, now alone, faced a street full of angry people. It must have looked to him like everybody in Boley had a gun and was headed his way—and that was substantially true.

He made it into the car, but then there was that stupid U-turn to make, and as he straightened out to head for the highway, one of the citizens calmly put a round through the windshield. Exit the driver, extinct. Patterson survived to face a long prison term.

Had Birdwell had the rudimentary forethought to park the getaway car facing the right direction, and run for it the moment the alarm went off, he just might have cleared the town alive.

The *Daily Oklahoman* and the governor, Alfalfa Bill Murray, made much of the triumph of law and order in Boley, and indeed, the people of the little town deserved it richly. Because of them, the area was a lot safer, for now the town had a reputation that would not be lost on other would-be bandits, not to mention the beneficial extermination of George Birdwell and company.

Then there was the Miller family, a close runner-up to the Smiddys, and the Bradshaws, a dense group who appear elsewhere in this book (see photograph on page 5). Deacon Jim Miller—also called Killer Miller—probably set the record for bad Millers ("I killed fifty-one men," he allegedly said just before he was lynched), but William "Billy the Baby Face Killer" Miller—no relation—runs him a very close second.

An Ohio boy, he was one of sixteen kids born to a laborer and his wife. Daddy Miller left this earth abruptly when Billy was twelve or thirteen; the father made the serious mistake of threatening to kill lawmen who were after him for chicken rustling. He reached for his weapon, but he found out that he'd brought a knife to a gunfight.

Billy turned to thievery—apparently he shared his dad's fondness for other people's chickens, but then he graduated to more costly things like cars. He was in company with one brother—Roy, a bootlegger—when officers blew his brother off into the next world. The next brother to go was Joe, and Billy saw to this one himself, apparently as the result of rivalry over a woman.

In 1926 another brother, Okey, was murdered by persons unknown, although Billy was again suspected, the cause thought to be a liquor deal gone bad. Two years later still another brother, Grover, was shot and wounded when he went along with Billy on a robbery. Billy went off to prison for that one—Grover escaped before trial—and while Billy was up the river, he joined Floyd—yes, another brother—doing time in the same pen. He was later part of a spectacular escape and went right back to robbing again.

Like Elmer McCurdy, whom we'll meet shortly, Al Jennings was a considerable embarrassment to the outlaw profession. And like Elmer, he embarked on a second career and was infinitely more successful than he had been as a bandit. The difference was that unlike Elmer he didn't have to get himself killed to change careers. And it helped that he was an expert at reinventing himself, producing not only reams of dubious prose but a movie glorifying his undistinguished past as a criminal.

Al was a braggart, but then a lot of criminals were. What really characterized him as an incompetent failure was his persistent blundering. Al was inept to an extent unusual even in a line of work in which intelligence was not a common virtue.

Christened Alphonso J. Jennings, he was born in 1863 back in Virginia, son of a lawyer. By 1892 his family had moved west and settled in the town of El Reno in Canadian County, Oklahoma Territory. His father became a judge in the local court, and Al practiced law in the area with his brothers, John and Ed.

Now in those days Territory lawyers tended to be a tough, aggressive bunch, and the Jennings boys fit right in. It was their misfortune, however, to meet one of the toughest of them all, Temple Houston. He was the son of Sam Houston, the father of Texas, and he had been both a district attorney and a state senator down in Brazoria County, a wild Panhandle judicial district.

Houston was the epitome of the successful frontier lawyer, with the Prince Albert coat, the ornate vest, and, of course, the Colt revolver. Then he moved north to Woodward, up in Oklahoma Territory, and it was there that he locked horns with the Jennings boys.

The conflict apparently arose over some harsh words exchanged in court during a hard-fought case involving Houston on one side and Ed and John Jennings representing the other. Houston

Al Jennings.

referred to brother Ed as "grossly ignorant of the law"—which he may well have been—at which Ed took umbrage, called him a liar, and started for him. Both men reached for their guns, but others prevented any bloodletting there and then.

Now that sort of thing was not uncommon in those days—what made the disagreement especially bad this time was that after court adjourned Houston and a sometime sheriff named Love met Ed and brother John in the Cabinet Saloon. One version of what happened then tells that Houston called, "Ed, I want to see you a minute," gesturing toward the back of the room. "See me here and now, you son of a bitch," said Ed, an unwise thing to say. All four men went for their guns, the saloon roared with gunfire, and the lights went out. When the smoke blew away, Ed ended up dead on the saloon floor and John fled for his life with wounds in his arm and body.

Al wrote later—he wrote a lot in later life—claiming that Ed was "ambushed." However, several territorial newspapers published accounts of the fight that indicate it was no more than a common brawl in which the Jennings brothers came in second.

> The quarrel was renewed. Very few words passed before all drew their pistols, including [Houston's friend] Love . . . All engaged in a running and dodging fight except Houston. The huge man stood up straight and emptied his revolver without twitching a muscle. . . . Neither Love nor Houston were wounded although several bullets passed through their clothes and hats.

Al wrote dramatically that he was summoned to the saloon, where he knelt beside his brother's corpse and "swore to kill the man who had murdered him."

But he didn't.

Instead, Love and Houston were duly tried and acquitted after eyewitnesses said Ed Jennings went for his gun first and it appeared he might have actually been shot by his own brother. In any case, Al fulminated a lot about killing Houston but continued to do nothing about it except work his mouth.

Instead of acting, he wired another brother, Frank, in Denver, and the two went "on the scout," as the saying went. "We could not trust ourselves in Woodward," Al wrote dramatically, "where Love and Houston would offer continual temptation."

This move to the sticks was, Al said later, to set up a lair from which to sally forth and kill Houston and Love. They weren't hard to find, but somehow the Jennings boys never managed to be where Houston and Love were at the same time. Instead, the Jennings boys launched their outlaw career, which turned out to be both undistinguished and unproductive.

They collected some helpers, Morris and Pat O'Malley, and somewhere along the way were joined by perennial Territory bad-man Little Dick West, alumnus of the Doolin gang. They may also have recruited Dan Clifton, better known by his outlaw handle of Dynamite Dick, a one-time Dalton and Doolin follower.

Early in June 1897 the new gang held up a store in Violet Springs, one of the infamous Pottawatomie County "saloon towns." They then went on to stick up another country store, robbed a "party of freighters" on the road, and then capped their spree by robbing another saloon and all the patrons. Carrying a sackful of money and some stolen whiskey, the little band headed for the woods to relax and enjoy both their whiskey and their success.

Robbers identified as Al and Dynamite Dick held up a post office at a wide spot in the road not far from the town of Claremore. That brought federal officers looking for them. In his whiny auto-biography, *Beating Back*, Al said this early raid was only to test out something called a "set-screw," a contraption, he said, that was designed to pop loose locks from safes. This robbery netted the gang seven hundred dollars, which Al said was stolen "just to pay expenses."

It was a good beginning, especially since everybody in the bunch was a tyro bandit except for Little Dick and Dynamite Dick. It was also the last major run of success the gang would have, and now the law was looking for them. Chief among the searchers were Deputy U.S. Marshals Paden Tolbert and Bud Ledbetter, who were not good men to have on your back trail. Both marshals were experienced, smart, and tough.

Al now got more ambitious. On the night of August 16, he and his cohorts stopped a Santa Fe train near Edmond, a town just north of Oklahoma City. Three members of the gang boarded the train at Ponca City, well to the north, and transferred to the tender when the train stopped for water at Edmond.

The outlaws then forced the train to halt a little way down the road, and four more men came out of the darkness to join the first three. There followed much shooting and yelling designed to keep the train's crew and passengers from interfering with the gang's onslaught on the express car. Bullets through the wall of the car forced the agents to open the door, and the gang entered to claim their bonanza.

So far, so good. But then things went sour. The set-screw apparently having been left behind or proven to be unsatisfactory, the gang tried dynamite. Not once but twice they blasted the Wells Fargo safe, but it refused to open. Defeated, the outlaws ordered the train crew to drive on and disappeared. Once the news was passed to the marshals, posses hit the road from both Guthrie and Kingfisher, but at last lost the track.

Empty-handed from their first try at a train, the gang decided to try it again a couple of weeks later. This time they chose a spot off to the east, a place called Bond Switch, not far from Muskogee.

Nobody tried to ride the train this time. Instead, the gang stacked railroad ties on the tracks and hunkered down to wait for their prey. The train arrived as scheduled, but the engineer, instead of jamming on the brakes and stopping, used the throttle, smashed through the barricade of ties, and disappeared into the night.

Unrobbed.

With the law again on their trail, the gang decided to replenish their money supply by robbing the Santa Fe train depot at Purcell, south of the town of Norman. This time they didn't even get started, for a night watchman saw them skulking about in the gloom before they managed to rob anything. The watchman promptly alerted the station agent. He called the city marshal, who showed up with a posse. The gang ran for it.

Curses, foiled again!

Shortly afterward, one story goes, the law learned that the gang intended to rob the bank in Minco, but the outlaws again were thwarted because a band of citizens mounted a twenty-four-hour guard on the bank. The gang was getting hungry.

About now considerable mythology surrounds the gang's operations. Al Jennings wrote long afterward that at this point he and Frank were comparatively rich from train robberies and a bank job down in Texas. Well, maybe. Rich or not, according to Jennings they took a six-month trip to Honduras. There they met one William Sydney Porter, better known later as O. Henry, who would go on to write dozens of the world's most memorable short stories. Just now, however, he was also on the run, facing an embezzlement rap in Texas.

Early in 1897 Porter came back to turn himself in and face the music, but Jennings, according to him anyway, returned to Texas by way of San Francisco and Mexico City. Whether Jennings was luxuriating in Honduras or not, or simply hiding out in penury, he was back with the old gang by October 1897 and preparing to try on another train.

This time the gang chose the Rock Island, selecting a southbound train they thought was carrying some ninety thousand dollars headed for banks in Fort Worth. Al decided to stop this train in broad daylight, on the thesis that the usual guards were only on duty at night. And so, on the morning of October 1, the gang—six men this time—forced a railroad section crew to stop the train. The gang hid themselves behind bandannas, except for Al, who had made himself a mask out of a bearskin saddle pocket, of all things, cutting a couple of eyeholes for visibility.

Again, a good beginning, and this time Al and his men had brought lots of dynamite. They were resolved not to be stopped again by a strong safe. And so they laid their charge, lit the fuse, and waited for the money. The explosives went off with a colossal roar, tearing the express car to pieces, but the safe remained intact. Along the way Al's grotesque mask slipped. Frustrated, the bandits laid another and even heavier charge, and the whole train shook.

But not the safe.

So the gang was reduced to tearing open the registered mail and robbing the train crew and the passengers—more than a hundred of them—of their cash and watches. Along the way one of the outlaws shot off a piece of ear from a passenger who was slow to cooperate, but he was the only casualty.

This unusual daylight robbery brought lawmen in swarms, several posses converging by train on the outlaws' probable escape route. In addition, the American Express Company and the Rock Island ponied up a reward, a total of eight hundred dollars a head for every outlaw, a good deal of money in those far-off days.

But again the gang got away, ending up circling back to a farm near El Reno, home of a farmer who was well-disposed to them. There they rested and split up their meager loot. Riding through the cold weather of late October, they moved east toward the town of Cushing, and there they sought sanctuary from the chill and an infusion of money at the home of one Lee Nutter.

They did this simply by waking Nutter, a merchant, shoving a pistol in his face, and demanding that he go to his store at the front of the building and give them his money. But there wasn't any, for Nutter had sent his store's receipts on to the bank in Guthrie.

So the gang had to make do with a couple of weapons and a measly fifteen dollars, a selection of coats and such from the store's stocks, a jug of whiskey, and a bunch of bananas. It was another failure, but it was as close to a success as the gang would ever have again.

Somewhere around Tulsa, real outlaws Dynamite Dick and Little Dick West left the gang, at last disgusted with all that work and danger and hardship for virtually no reward. Then the two split up, and Dynamite Dick headed in the direction of Checotah. Early one morning he rode past two deputy marshals, Hess Bussey and George Lawson, lying in ambush waiting for him to appear.

The marshals offered Dick a chance to surrender, but he was wanted for more than the Jennings gang's amateurish crimes. There was a warrant for him for a murder committed back in his days with the Doolin gang. And so, with nothing to lose, the outlaw whipped up his Winchester and fired. A return shot broke his arm and knocked him from the saddle, but he regained his feet and staggered into the brush, leaving his rifle behind him.

The marshals followed, trailing him by spatters of blood, but the trail was hard to stick to. And then, as night fell and it seemed they had lost him completely, they came upon a cabin in the woods. Nobody answered their summons to surrender, until they fired warning shots and announced that they intended to burn the cabin to the ground.

At this an Indian woman and a boy came out. The officers twice commanded them to set fire to the cabin, and on the second command Dynamite Dick ran from the door, shooting as he came. The officers quickly put several holes in him, and he was dead within minutes.

Thus passed Dynamite Dick, veteran of dozens of outlaw forays including the fight at Ingalls, Oklahoma Territory, in which three deputy marshals died, as well as the bank holdup and murder at Southwest City, Missouri.

Little Dick West was next, still free and still wanted. Heartily sick of the inept Jennings and his crew, West agreed to help the law entrap the gang, which was again planning to rob a gold shipment. The gang had assembled at the ranch owned by Red Hereford, but left at the high lope just before the marshals' posse arrived.

This only delayed the reckoning a little. On November 29, 1897, the gang was holed up near Red Fork, ensconced in a ranch house on the Spike S Ranch owned by one John Harless. After they had eaten the evening meal, they were visited by a neighbor. He had been sent by the law to confirm the bandits' presence at the Harless place, but he was obviously nervous and somewhat unconvincingly claimed that he was lost.

Mrs. Harless didn't believe him and the bandits took alarm. They posted one of their number as a sentry in a wagon near the barn, but none of them—including their sentry—saw the federal posse surrounding the house in the darkness. Veteran deputy marshals Paden Tolbert and Bud Ledbetter were out there in the night with five other men, simply biding their time until the house grew dark and quiet.

The sentry proved to be a weak reed, for Bud Ledbetter appeared out of the gloom, threw down on him, and left him bound and gagged in the barn. On the morning of November 30, Mrs. Harless's son appeared, walking out to fetch a bucket of water. He entered the barn and the officers snapped him up to join the inept sentry. But Harless was missed around the family hearth, of course, and soon Mrs. Harless herself appeared and went into the barn. Ledbetter collared her and explained the situation.

"We have a warrant for Al Jennings," said Ledbetter. "I want you to go back inside and tell the outlaws they're surrounded. They are to come out with their hands up and surrender. If they don't, you and your hired girl leave the house at once and go to the cemetery." Mrs. Harless delivered her message, and Ledbetter could hear the sounds of argument from inside the house. Very quickly Mrs. Harless and the girl left the house, swathed in blankets against the cold.

And Jennings opened fire, but this time he and his men were up against the first team. Within a few minutes they realized it was time to flee. And so they did, running out the back of the cabin, heading for an orchard, and scrambling through fire from two possemen. They were lucky. One peace officer's rifle jammed at the first shot. A second got a charge of shot into Frank Jennings without appreciably slowing him down. All of the bandits had been wounded, but none were so crippled that they could not run at least a little way.

Al Jennings had been hit three times, including a bullet in his left thigh, but he could still move, and the bandits waded a creek and disappeared. Ledbetter was not happy, and even less so when the officers lost the trail and could not regain it after a long search.

Taking Morris O'Malley and the gang's horses and horse furniture with them, the posse returned to Muskogee.

The fleeing gang members got some transportation when they encountered two Indian boys in a wagon and commandeered both wagon and boys. The next day, after wandering somewhat aimlessly around the countryside, they stopped at the home of Willis Brooks, who sent them on to somebody called Sam Baker. The gang may have been free, but they were in sad shape otherwise. Al and Pat O'Malley, at least, needed medical attention, and Brooks went into Checotah to find a doctor.

He also found Bud Ledbetter and told him where the gang was hiding. And so that night Ledbetter, Tolbert, and two other lawmen set up an ambush in a ravine where the road passed beneath high banks. They dropped a tree across the road as a barricade and settled in to wait.

They waited most of the night until a wagon came creaking out of the gloom with Al and O'Malley bedded down in the back and Frank driving. Brooks had given them directions that were supposed to take them to safety in Arkansas. In fact, he sent them straight into Ledbetter's trap. There was no fight this time. Looking down the bores of four rifles, the outlaws gave it up and were transported on to the Muskogee jail, where Morris O'Malley already languished.

This left Little Dick West, still free, still wanted. West had friends in the Territory, so he could often find a safe place to hole up. Moreover, he had long been famous for wanting to sleep out-of-doors whatever the weather, someplace out in the brush away from people. He would be hard to catch.

But the law managed it, the law this time in the person of tough deputy U.S. marshal Heck Thomas, who had kept order in the Territory for long years and killed Bill Doolin when the outlaw leader would not heed his order to surrender. If anybody could run West down, it would be Thomas.

West was now working as a farmhand between Kingfisher and Guthrie, laboring for two different farmers, Fitzgerald and Arnett.

The wife of one farmer, Mrs. Arnett, spilled the beans when she was heard to say in Guthrie that Fitzgerald's hired hand was trying to get her husband to commit a robbery with him. Such evil tidings quickly found their way to Heck Thomas. While the hired man used an alias when he hired on, Thomas guessed from his description that he was hearing about Little Dick West.

Accordingly, on the seventh of April Thomas led a four-man posse, including the formidable Bill Tilghman, off to the Fitzgerald farm. Fitzgerald said he didn't know anything about the hired man, who in any event had long since left his employ. When the lawmen found in Fitzgerald's barn a horse matching the description of West's mount, the farmer said that he had traded for the animal.

Unconvinced, the posse rode off toward the Arnett place, and on the way they got lucky, spotting a man "scouting along the timber to the left." Thomas and Tilghman began to follow him, and the other three members of the posse rode on toward Arnett's. There they saw the same man standing by a shed. The man promptly stepped behind the barn and ran for it, and the three lawmen stepped into the open and ordered him to halt.

It was West, and his only response was to keep running and snap off several shots from his revolver. The lawmen responded with shotgun and rifle fire and West was hit as he dived under the bottom strand of a barbed-wire fence. He was dead before the possemen could reach him.

Now Al Jennings could start his second career, having been a notable flop at the first one. First, though, he had to go off to prison for a while. There is a story that Temple Houston magnanimously offered to defend Al, an offer somewhat ungratefully refused. And so in 1899 the court gave him a life term, later reduced to five years, allegedly through the legal talent of his brother John. He was released in 1902 and received a presidential pardon five years later.

Jennings settled in Oklahoma City in 1911, went back to practicing law, and almost immediately set his sights on political office. In 1912 he won nomination for county attorney of Oklahoma County, but lost in the general election. Nothing daunted, two years later he ran for governor, of all things, even openly talking a lot about his outlaw days.

By then his life on the scout was commemorated not only by his pompous 1913 book, *Beating Back*, but also by the film made from the book, also called *Beating Back*. Al even starred in the movie, which at least gave him great face recognition with the voters.

It wasn't enough. The best Al could do was finish third in a field of six in the Democratic primary. That was enough politics for him, so Al gave up both politics and the practice of law and retired to sunny California, where he went to work making western films. He died in Tarzana, California, on the day after Christmas, 1961. It had been quite a life.

Then there was the champion outlaw oaf of all time, which is saying a good deal. His name was Elmer McCurdy.

As a general rule, criminals are not overly bright, but once in a great while one comes along who is far stupider than the average. Elmer McCurdy was one of that distinguished few. He didn't amount to a tinker's damn as an outlaw, but he gets a little space because of his remarkable second career.

Elmer was, as the kids say, dumber than a rock, and not much of a criminal either. He ended up dead early in his criminal career, but that was not unusual in the world of western holdup men.

But Elmer didn't stay buried. Instead, he embarked on a whole new career, long and reasonably successful. His new occupation fit his intellect and personality: He became a professional dummy.

Literally.

Elmer was born in Maine and came west around the turn of the century. Although he worked for a while at ordinary jobs, Elmer was born to be an outlaw. Among other things he was a killer, and a jailbird with a string of aliases.

In the spring of 1911, Elmer and some others held up a train near Coffeyville, Kansas, just north of the Oklahoma line. This successful raid moved Elmer to lay plans for a holdup of the Missouri-Kansas-Texas Railroad.

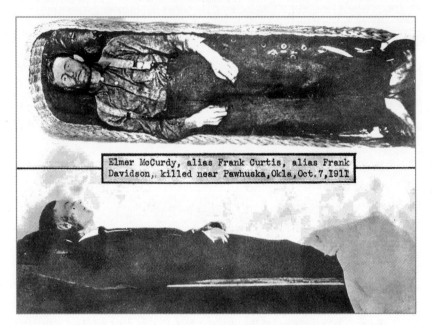

Elmer McCurdy, alias Frank Curtis, alias Frank Davidson, killed near Pawhuska, Okla, Oct. 7, 1911

Elmer McCurdy—on his second career.

OKLAHOMA UNIVERSITY WESTERN HISTORY LIBRARY

Elmer planned to strike a Katy train that carried thousands of dollars, maybe hundreds of thousands, periodic payments from the United States to various Indian tribes in Oklahoma. Elmer's plan was ambitious, but his execution was rotten.

On October 6, 1911, Elmer and his little gang of hoodlums stopped Katy train number 29 at night near Okesa, out in northeast Oklahoma. The gang uncoupled the engine and the express car from the rest of the train and moved them on down the line. So far, so good. Now it was time to reap the coveted bonanza they had waited for.

Wrong. Elmer had stopped the wrong train. Mean-spirited Elmer stole the conductor's watch and two demijohns of whiskey and departed—on foot—into the Osage Hills, of which, in 1911, the *Bartlesville* (Oklahoma) *Daily Enterprise* said:

[E]scaped criminals are able to disappear for days at a time, regardless of the advances civilization made during the past two or three years . . . the district outside of the developed oil belt contains every element of wildness that it did in the old territory days.

Elmer grew more and more spifflicated as he fled, steadily working on the whiskey stolen from the train. A posse on his trail found one of the demijohns, empty. That told them they weren't dealing with the smartest hen in the coop, and after a two-day chase, the pursuers caught up with Elmer at a farm out on the Big Caney River.

Elmer arrived at the farm drunker than a skunk, as the old-timers said. He spent some time drinking with some ranch hands before he finally headed for the barn to seek solace in sleep. While he was in dreamland, three Osage deputies appeared and wisely decided not to go poking into a dark barn after an armed outlaw.

And so they waited. With daylight Elmer looked outside and made his last mistake: He reached for his Winchester.

A more intelligent thief would probably have surrendered, for he hadn't killed anybody during his botched holdup and so wasn't in danger of the rope. Not dense Elmer. He traded shots with the posse for an hour or so until at last a lawman's bullet tore through the right side of Elmer's chest and bored on through his body, all the way into the lower abdomen, killing him quite dead.

That should have been the end of the line for Elmer. After all, he was a nobody among Oklahoma outlaws. Still, Elmer was just embarking on a new career, and everybody has to start someplace.

The posse hauled Elmer's remains into Pawhuska and handed him over to the ministrations of Johnson's undertaking emporium. Sensing a windfall in a town where not very much exciting happened, the mortician preserved Elmer with an arsenic compound that ossified him into a sort of unwrapped mummy. He was stored in the back room of the undertaking parlor and the enterprising owner charged the general public a nickel to look at him.

Elmer wasn't famous, but a five-cent outlaw was better than no outlaw at all. Elmer was featured as "The Bandit Who Wouldn't Give Up," and he hung around—or stood around—Pawhuska until about 1916.

Until a tearful visitor approached the undertaker and announced that Elmer was his long-lost brother. Give me back my kin, the stranger pleaded, so I can bury him in the family plot. The undertaker took pity on the grieving visitor and handed what was left of Elmer over to him.

Not until too late did he learn that Elmer's "brother" was no relation at all. The man ran a carnival, and Elmer was off to new adventures. Elmer apparently wasn't much of an attraction on the road, and so he sat around in movie theater lobbies as a come-on for a variety of western films, and spent a couple of decades in storage in between jobs.

As the years went by, Elmer passed from hand to hand, traveling for a while with Sonney's Museum of Crime, a sort of mobile waxworks. In time, Elmer moved on to Craft's Carnival Circus, finally ending up in something named the Hollywood Wax Museum in the Nu-Pike Amusement Park. By this time, covered with wax and showing his age, Elmer was featured as "The One-Thousand-Year-Old Man."

When the Hollywood Wax Museum went out of business, Elmer had a chance to appear in the Mount Rushmore Haunted House, but he failed his audition when it developed he had grown stiff as a plank with the years.

Elmer ended up the property of the owner of the Nu-Pike park, who painted Elmer with a concoction that glowed orange and red under ultraviolet light and hung him up with a hangman's noose in a exhibit called "The Laugh in the Dark Fun House."

Elmer's great moment finally came through television, in an episode of *The Six Million Dollar Man*. Setting up for a camera shot, a crew member moved what appeared to be a dummy dangling forlornly in a noose.

As the dummy was moved, its arm fell off, and the technicians found they had partially disassembled a real human being. It was indeed. It was Elmer.

The Los Angeles County coroner, Dr. Thomas Noguchi, was no stranger to bizarre, high-profile cases, this being Southern California. Still, this John Doe, Number 255, was a different kind of case altogether. Mummies don't show up every day, even in Los Angeles.

The examiner checked the cause of death as "homicide," which it plainly was. But he also checked the box showing the death occurred "not at work." He did not know then that Elmer had indeed been at work when he met his end. Elmer wasn't very good at what he did, but he was trying.

Incisions in what was left of Elmer told the examiner that Elmer had been professionally embalmed. And he was full of arsenic, a substance that embalmers had generally ceased to use about 1920. That gave the investigators a broad but workable window in time.

The cause of death provided more help. The slug that killed Elmer was not recovered, but its copper jacket was, and it was enough to identify the caliber of the round as .32-20. Now, manufacture of the .32-20 stopped before World War II, and the copper jacket first appeared on American ammunition in about 1905.

So, between the bullet caliber, the copper jacket, and the arsenic embalming, the investigators had narrowed the time of Elmer's death to a window of about fifteen years.

And then an alert examiner noted that Elmer's mouth contained items not usually found in such places, notably a 1924 penny and some ticket stubs, one of which was printed "Louis Sonney's Museum of Crime, So. Main St., L.A." The coroner could now trace Elmer's travels, working backward across the years.

The last of Elmer's owners, Ed Liersch, said he'd gotten Elmer from a Mr. Singh at the Hollywood Wax Museum. One Dave Friedman, described as a Hollywood filmmaker, said the Sonney company owned Elmer until it sold him to the Hollywood Museum in 1968. Elmer had been dusted off in 1964, put back into service, and re-exhibited. He even appeared in an eminently forgettable Friedman epic called *She Freak*.

"It's old Elmer, all right," said Friedman. "I'm surprised no one ever fixed his arm on properly. It's been falling off for years."

Louis Sonney, whose ticket stub ended up in Elmer's mouth, had bought Elmer forty or fifty years before, exhibiting him under his real name. After Sonney's death Elmer was stored with other dubious attractions in a Los Angeles warehouse, until he was acquired by Singh twenty-two years later.

Finally, one Dwayne Esper said he'd gotten Elmer in about 1926 from "a retired coroner in Tulsa, Oklahoma," and that he was "an outlaw, shot in the early 1900's in a small town near Tulsa."

The investigator added his own small spot of macabre comedy to the McCurdy saga: "The cadaver had supposedly robbed a bank in a small town near Tulsa, Oklahoma."

Which sounds a little like a bad horror film.

Finally, forensic anthropologist Dr. Clyde Snow flew from Oklahoma to examine Elmer and found a scar on the cadaver's wrist in a spot where Elmer was known to have a similar scar. Then he went high-tech, with a pair of video cameras linked to a special-effects generator and wired to a monitor. One camera showed the mummy in profile. The other projected a 1911 postmortem photograph of Elmer, also in profile.

The two profiles, overlapped, matched very closely. The profile match, along with the considerable accumulation of other hard evidence, was enough to conclude that the mummy was indeed Elmer, in the flesh, as it were. All of this fuss had made him something of a celebrity, even in blasé California. He even made *NBC News*, appearing in person, though he didn't say much.

Elmer returned to Oklahoma in April 1977, guest of the Oklahoma Historical Society and the Indian Territory Posse of Westerners, a body of public-spirited Oklahomans who aim to preserve the state's considerable historical heritage.

Elmer had a first-class funeral, drawn to his last rest in a gentle rain, resting in an antique horse-drawn hearse, the kind that had glass windows in the sides so you could catch a last glimpse of the departed. He got a mounted escort from the Westerners and a lot better eulogy than he deserved.

Now Elmer awaits the Last Trumpet in the cemetery at Guthrie, once the state capital. He has a decent memorial and also a couple of cubic yards of concrete on top of him to discourage the morbid from disturbing Elmer's rest.

His grave is not far from that of Bill Doolin, a real outlaw, and he is surrounded by an assortment of pioneers, outlaws, and politicians, which perhaps suggested this bit of doggerel, the last word on Elmer McCurdy:

> Rest in peace, dear Elmer,
> Beneath this Okie sky,
> Where many an outlaw slumbers,
> And politicians lie.

Chapter 9

TYPHOID MARY

The Bloody Trail of Al Spencer

AL SPENCER HAD A longer-than-usual run, although he was a sort of Typhoid Mary to his colleagues, who became extinct or confined in considerable numbers. Joining Al's band of failures was usually a quick ticket to prison or the morgue, at a rate even higher than the rest of the outlaw world.

Al robbed a lot of things and people; he may rival Henry Starr for the lead in number of banks held up, somewhere between twenty and forty. But he was, however, the consummate fumbler, much given to stupidities of the most avoidable kind. Hence the mortality rate among his followers.

Al was born in 1887 near Lenapah in Oklahoma. Early on he worked as a farmer and cowboy, but by 1916 he was busy cattle rustling. He did some successful automobile rustling as well, until in 1919 he was part of a store burglary in Neodesha, Kansas. This one didn't go so well, especially the escape, due to Al's stupid idea of sending a telegram to a friend, asking him to send money to a place in Colorado.

Detectives from the Burns Agency read his wire, and when Al went to the post office to pick up his money, he found a set of handcuffs instead. This one got him five years. Since Oklahoma was waiting for him on a rustling charge, he was returned there, where he got a stretch at McAlester penitentiary. So far Al was batting about zero, but it didn't change his preference for the dark side.

When Al got out, he went back to what he liked to do: take things that belonged to other folks. After rustling some more cars, he stuck up the assistant postmaster of a small town as that worthy was walking home from a poker game. Al bungled it and got some serious time, fourteen years back in McAlester, where he became a "trusty," a convict trusted not to run and allowed considerable freedom of movement.

Then in 1921 or early in 1922, still intent on being the master criminal, Al went AWOL. When somebody missed Al and asked where he was, another prisoner said he was probably drinking in a "choc joint," choc being a sort of beer. It was a practice actually condoned by the prison authorities as long as you were a trusty. The lie bought Al enough time to get away and return to his outlaw career, which so far was nothing to write home about.

This time he would concentrate on banks. After all, that was, as Willie Sutton said later, where the money was. Al was raising his aspirations. In December 1921 a former confederate called Silas Meigs held up the bank in Nelagony, a hamlet on the fringe of the Osage Hills in northeastern Oklahoma. He got some fifteen hundred dollars single-handedly and, in the best western tradition, galloped off to safety.

That looked good to Al, so he joined Meigs in robbing the bank in Pawhuska, taking away a paltry $147.60. Then, still in February, they hit the bank in Broken Bow, and this time they struck it rich, something between six and seven thousand dollars. They forced a local man to drive them out of town to a spot where they had stashed their horses. Then they galloped away, eluding another posse, but their budding sense of self-satisfaction was not to last.

They hid out for a while up in the tangled wilderness of the Osage Hills, an area with a rich tradition of use as a shelter for bad men hunted by the law. Even Pretty Boy Floyd was often a denizen of the Osage. One old-timer said of Spencer what would be true of others on the run, that it was "like a game of hide and seek . . . to try to capture him."

Al and Meigs must have felt safe, but that was not to last, for a posse came upon them at Sol Wells' place. The lawmen were hunting a still somewhere in the area, but as they neared the outlaws' lair, Meigs shot and killed a posseman. The return fire did for Meigs, the first of a number of Al's associates who would finish their earthly course on the wrong end of a bullet.

Nothing daunted by the ventilation of Meigs, Al teamed up with other outlaws, Jay Majors and Slim Connelly. Their target was a bank in little Pineville, Missouri, in the spring of 1922. First the four hung around the area for a while, doing some fishing and presumably casing the bank. Then, in an act of colossal stupidity, they robbed a local bootlegger instead of merely buying the booze they wanted. That brought out the law, who stopped a car carrying three men and a woman, one Eva Evers.

The lawmen were immediately in a gunfight with the occupants, and in the exchange of shots, Majors took a round in the groin. The outlaws took Majors to a Joplin hospital and dropped him there, where, not surprisingly, the law soon found him. They also found Eva and arrested her as well.

Spencer got away, riding a freight train back down into Oklahoma and refuge back in the Osage Hills. About now Connelly quit the gang, to be replaced by young Dick Gregg.

In early June 1922 the outlaws set out to burgle a store in Ochelata, but this time they were stopped by the night marshal, William Lockett. The bandits killed Lockett, one of them saying, "You've followed us long enough, you old bastard." Gregg may have done the shooting, but there is some evidence that Spencer was the killer.

The Elgin State Bank, just over the border in Kansas, was a better strike. There the gang got about two thousand dollars in cash, plus a bundle of bonds with a face value of about twenty thousand. Then, at the end of July, four outlaws hit the Citizens' Bank of Lenapah—Al's hometown—and got away with about thirteen hundred dollars. They wore masks, but the odds are that Al was in on the crime.

In October 1922 Al was probably part of a bank robbery at Osage. This time there were five robbers, and two of them were women, or maybe men inexplicably dressed as women. This may have been the first appearance of Goldie Bates, Spencer's girlfriend.

On the eighteenth of October, the bank at Dewey lost some twenty-five hundred dollars to three bandits, who locked the bank personnel in the vault. The robbers were spotted in a fast Hudson Speedster, allegedly driven by a woman—which could be Goldie again—but got away clean.

Until, that is, one of the bank men picked Henry Wells out of a photo lineup. But Wells had—or created—an alibi backed up by witnesses, and his lawyer got a hung jury. For law-abiding people worse was to follow, for on October 20 Majors and other prisoners broke out of the Vinita jail during a nearby revival meeting, forced passing drivers to halt, and disappeared into the night in stolen cars.

Still in October, Spencer and two others hit the Talala bank for twelve hundred dollars or so and fled back to the wilds of the Osage. By now Al had recruited some more bad hats, a juvenile delinquent named Ralph Clopton and one Emmett Daugherty, said to be somehow related to the dean of bank robbers, Henry Starr. Also added to the pack was Dick Gregg's buddy Lee Clingan.

On Armistice Day the gang killed a lawman in Independence, Kansas, when officers surprised the bandits in the midst of looting a clothing store. The fatal shot was probably fired by one of Spencer's newer men, a punk called Jesse Paul, whose nom de crime was Big Boy Berry.

Then, on December 2, the gang stuck up a bank in Towanda, Kansas, making off with a couple of thousand in cash and some twenty thousand in bonds. Two weeks later three gang members got more cash from the Caddo National Bank down in Oklahoma.

On the nineteenth the gang made themselves some Christmas presents at a jewelry store up in Kansas, fleeing in the now-familiar Hudson Speedster. This time they struck it rich—by their standards—making off with jewelry and watches worth as much as twenty thousand dollars.

But the tide was beginning to turn against Spencer and his minions. The day after Christmas a posse rounded up Majors, who would get twenty-one years.

Al was a famous outlaw by now, and he wasn't about to stop. Robberies followed at banks in Virgil and Cambridge, Kansas. After the Cambridge raid the gang fled to Oklahoma, driving across fields and through fences on the way. Inevitably they got chunks of fence stuck in a tangle of wire, and when they tried to free the car, a pursuing posse shot up the car and wounded Clopton, Daugherty, and a hostage.

Clopton became a prisoner and lost no time in telling the law that Spencer was the gang leader. Clopton got fifteen years, and passes from the stage. After this latest debacle the gang hid out for a month or so, and then robbed another Kansas bank in a place called Chautauqua. Wells was arrested for this one, but bank employees could not identify him as one of the robbers.

In March things turned really ugly. In Bartlesville, Oklahoma, an automobile passed the home of the police chief, named Gaston, and somebody fired on the house. It was Spencer, although he was not identified as the shooter until much later. In the same month the gang hit a bank in a village called Manford, west of Tulsa, taking a disappointing six hundred dollars.

They were pursued by a posse and had to abandon their car when they blew a tire. One of the outlaws, a Tulsa man called Leo Sturtz, was captured while he was vainly trying to change the tire. And the next day still another outlaw went down in a firefight with lawmen. The dead bandit turned out to be one Bud Maxfield, a veteran badman who in years past had ridden with Henry Starr. Spencer may or may not have been part of this raid.

The gang's next foray was into Arkansas, where they robbed the bank in Gentry, driving one car and leaving another just across the line in Oklahoma. The idea was that they would flee Gentry in one car, return to Oklahoma to swap the first car for the second one, and finally head for the tall timber on horseback.

Spencer's crew probably included Wells, Big Boy Berry, Nick Lamar, and Ralph White. Included as horse holder was somebody named Si Fogg—although the holder might also have been Red Cloud Scruggs. If it was Scruggs, it didn't matter long, for he was killed during another holdup about a year afterward.

And so, on March 31, 1923, Spencer and his crew arrived in Gentry driving a new Studebaker, stolen of course. While White waited behind the wheel, the other three went inside and snatched a little over two thousand dollars. But a bank employee hit the silent alarm, and when the gang headed for their car, citizens with guns were converging on the bank. Bullets began to fly, and Al and his boys ran for it. They weren't used to tough citizens.

The gang roared out of town, right into an ambush two or three miles down the road. Firing from behind a stone wall in a small village, lawmen and citizens drilled Lamar in the shoulder and legs, White in his arms and side, and Spencer in one arm. The car was riddled, but the outlaws got to their horses and rode away, taking refuge at the home of a confederate named Reasor.

Three lawmen showed up at Reasor's place, and still another firefight ensued. One officer was wounded, and the shot-up bandits had to jump on their horses and again make a run for it. The law arrested Reasor, Campbell Keyes, and another man and found a stolen car stashed in Reasor's barn.

The bandits went to ground in a cemetery, from which Spencer walked into town and telephoned Stanley Snyder in Bartlesville. Snyder and another man picked up the battered outlaws and drove them to the relative safety of the Osage. It hadn't been much of a day for Al and the boys.

On the night of April 16, the gang hit the post office in Pawhuska. They threw down on a deputy U.S. marshal named Tom

Walton as he walked over to talk to them and then forced a cab driver down on the pavement beside the lawman. Some of the men stood guard while the others broke into the post office.

All was quiet until two citizens passed, Harrison and Wilkerson, a special policeman. Unsuspecting, the men were walking peacefully homeward in the darkness when one of the bandits yelled at the two and then cut Harrison down with a shotgun. Wilkerson tried to draw his pistol, but he went down from a second shotgun blast.

A woman with the gang saw the outlaw's stupid act for what it was: disaster. "You ignorant bastard," she yelled, "you've shot two innocent men and now there'll be hell to pay." There would be.

About then the night lit up with a colossal explosion inside the post office building. The outlaws had dynamited the post office safe, using a charge heavy enough to hurl the outer safe door thirty feet. It immediately appeared that Al and his cohorts weren't very good at handling explosives, for what the mighty blast also did was jam the inner door so tight that it sealed off the contents of the safe and the robbers got nothing. They ran then, spraying bullets indiscriminately in all directions, leaped into their cars, and roared off toward Bartlesville.

Wilkerson died later that night when doctors could not halt the bleeding from his torn femoral artery. He was in his early twenties, and the next day would have been his wedding day. Harrison would survive. Officers from all directions joined in the hunt. Robbery was one thing; cold-blooded murder was quite another.

And the law hit pay dirt the next day at a house near Ochelata. While two officers were questioning the people living there, one of the bandits stupidly opened fire on them from his hiding place in the attic overhead. A return volley from the lawmen produced the almost instant surrender of a thug known as Ed Shull—shot through the leg—and Clarence Ward. The two gang members had a small arsenal in the house, and Shull was already wanted for assault on an officer and suspected in two robberies.

Frightened of being lynched—a well-founded fear—Shull spilled his guts. On his information lawmen raided Sol Wells' home, where they put the arm on Earl Holman, another gang member. Holman would get thirty years and Shull five, his lighter sentence a thank-you for the information he had furnished. Clarence Ward lost his leg to amputation and was charged with the Caddo bank robbery.

Though the civilized world was well rid of Shull and company, they may not have been involved in the post office raid. That was attributed to Spencer and his gang, and Spencer himself was identified as the probable killer of Wilkerson.

At last, on April 21, Spencer was spotted in a stolen car with a woman and three other men. A posse ran down the automobile, loaded with weapons and camping equipment but now abandoned, and not far away they found outlaw Nick Lamar, spattered with buckshot. Lamar did not try to reach his weapons.

Then, on May 4, Texas lawmen stopped a stolen car and arrested Goldie Bates, Spencer's inamorata, plus Big Boy Berry and one Carl Priss, described as a Texas horse thief. Goldie and Priss were later released, there being no valid charges to hold them on. Lamar and Berry, having admitted participation in the Gentry robbery, got some serious prison time from the court in Benton County, Arkansas. So did Keyes and Reasor, for the same crime.

Instead of running for safety, leaving Oklahoma, or holing up in the Osage, Spencer demonstrated his abysmal lack of judgment and took on a train. He was accompanied by Frank "Jelly" Nash, later to be killed in the Kansas City Union Station massacre; Earl Thayer, a long-time criminal; and a small army of other outlaws, including Riley Dixon, Curtis Kelly, Grover Durrill, and Whitey Fallon (born plain old George Curtis).

Spencer's band of boobies had earlier demonstrated their intellectual poverty by driving around western Arkansas with a jug of nitroglycerine, covered with a blanket, sitting on the running board of their car. Suddenly discovering that the blanket was inexplicably on fire, they got rid of the explosive.

The train didn't pan out. They only got a couple of thousand in cash from the express car. They couldn't get in to rob the passengers, thanks to the Pullman porter, a tough black man named T.J. Davis. Davis got the coach doors locked and tried to find somebody among the passengers who had a gun. Nobody did, or at least nobody would admit he did. Davis was disgusted and said so: "I suppose they were all from Kansas. They sure wasn't from Oklahoma, or they would all have had gats."

The bandits climbed into three cars and roared away into the night. Their satisfaction with an unusually large haul would not last long.

There is a persistent story that on this job Al won a measure of brief fame as the man who used rubber fingerstalls—rubber fingertip covers—to frustrate the burgeoning art of fingerprint identification. Al figured his ploy would keep his fingerprints off anything he touched during another robbery of a Katy train. It did. But what he didn't figure on were some bright Katy detectives who asked around to find out who'd been buying lots of fingerstalls.

In fact, the story seems to be true, except that the notion came from one of Al's confederates, an oaf called Ike Ogg. Ike was quickly arrested and began forthwith to sing.

The law swept up a passel of well-known Osage bad men and also netted Goldie Bates again, who was taken to Pawhuska dressed in "flaming red" stockings beneath a short dress. Goldie was feisty as always, fighting the officers who arrested her. While nearly all of those arrested this day would later be released as not involved in the train holdup, Ogg pleaded guilty.

Officers got Earl Thayer at home in Oklahoma City and netted Curtis Kelly on the thirtieth. He gave the lawmen all the information they needed, and by September 8 the world was told the names of the gang members, given their descriptions, and advised that each carried a substantial reward—dead or alive. Spencer was named, as was Riley "Pug" Dixon, Grover Durrill, Jelly Nash, and George Fallon. The handwriting was on the wall.

Spencer's luck had been in up to now, but on the fifteenth of September, U.S. Marshal Alva McDonald set up an ambush along a road they had been told Spencer would use. It was a cold, rainy night, and the officers—including tough Luther Bishop, one of the most lethal cops of his time—huddled in the darkness waiting for their target to appear. It was a long wait, but finally they saw Spencer crossing a bridge and moving in their direction.

McDonald said later that he challenged Spencer, but the outlaw fired twice in the darkness. The posse's return fire punctured Al eight times. As usual, there were a number of versions of precisely what happened on that gloomy road, but there was no argument with the fact that Spencer was very dead.

A newspaper story reported that Spencer had double-crossed his partners in crime and kept more than his share of loot. A sometime admirer of the outlaw leader, one Snyder, may have lured Al from his hideout after discovering that the outlaw leader had played his comrades false. Snyder had some hard words for his former idol:

> No friend of Spencer would walk two feet to avenge his
> death. He was too cheap . . . After J.C. Majors was convicted
> . . . I asked him to give me some money to send to Mrs.
> Majors, who was in destitute circumstances. He refused to
> give anything and said he couldn't see his way to give any-
> thing to help any man who was fool enough to get caught.

Some people speculated that the lawmen had killed Spencer in Kansas. Others said it happened in Oklahoma. Wells said Snyder himself had killed Spencer, shooting him in the back with his own shotgun. In this version the undertaker is supposed to have told Wells that Spencer still had food in his mouth, and Wells claimed that after Snyder had killed Spencer, "a bunch of officers . . . must have shot his body full of holes."

Whatever happened, Al Spencer remained dead.

He was planted in a cemetery outside Nowata on a soggy day in September 1923. For all his notoriety, nobody cared enough to come. Only his wife and daughter, his sister, and Campbell Keyes showed up to say goodbye.

Part of the sequel was the conviction of Fallon, Thayer, Durrill, and Curtis Casey. Stanley Snyder beat his wife once too often, and in 1926 she filled him full of a fatal dose of bullets. Dick Gregg got ten to twenty up in Kansas, but escaped and went back to robbing again. He got some help and hit some more banks, and then capped his ugly career not far from Tulsa by shooting down two Oklahoma highway patrolmen. One of the officers killed Gregg in the gunfight, but both troopers would also die.

Other relics of the Spencer gang broke out of prison in 1931. With some other prisoners Earl Thayer, Grover Durrill, and George Curtis reached freedom and then managed to make every mistake they possibly could, including getting their car stuck and failing in their efforts to hijack two more. Their escape attempt came unglued within ten miles of the prison.

Four of the escapees, including Thayer, took refuge in a farmhouse, which was surrounded by the law, as many as two hundred officers. Three of them went upstairs and tried to make a fight of it, but there was no place to hide, no way to run. After a lengthy bombardment the officers cautiously approached the farmhouse and found Durrell, Curtis, and the third man, Green, all quite dead, apparently suicides.

The canny Thayer had bailed out a back window early in the action, but his success was fleeting. He attracted the suspicion of a couple of civilians, who pulled a gun on him and called the police. Back to prison he went, and there he died in July 1934.

And so passed Al Spencer and the gaggle of losers called the Spencer gang, either into prison or into the grave. None of them had ever learned a thing.

Chapter 10

THE FEMALE OF THE SPECIES

"THE FEMALE OF THE SPECIES is more deadly than the male," wrote Rudyard Kipling. Though that great poet was seldom wrong about people, he missed the mark when his dictum was applied to the ladies of the Old West. Tales of woman bandits abound, but there were surprisingly few who lived up to their billing. Scarlet ladies there were in abundance, but the ancient and honorable profession of whoring is a very different thing from shooting people and robbing them.

First, a little of the mythology, which is a great deal more interesting, as usual, than the unvarnished truth.

An enduring female outlaw legend is the tale of the lady called the Rose of Cimarron, whose story will be forever tied to the Doolin gang. There was probably a Rose, sure enough, a woman named Rosa Dunn, sister to a pair of brothers who worked both sides of the law. Legend says that in the wild battle at Ingalls, Oklahoma Territory, between the Doolin gang and a party of lawmen, she shinnied down a rope of sheets from a second-floor window, first lowering a rifle and ammunition for her light of love, a professional hoodlum called Bittercreek Newcomb.

Picture that. With bullets flying in all directions, this girl is performing a very difficult climbing maneuver and somehow lowering a rifle and cartridges, too. Then, says one version of her story, she helps the injured Newcomb mount, leaps up in front of him, and gallops away. Version B of that tale is that she gets a horse, leads the animal to Newcomb, helps her outlaw lover mount, and then slaps the horse on the fanny and watches it carry Newcomb to safety.

Sadly, residents of Ingalls at the time of fight didn't know the Rose, and at least one opined that Bittercreek didn't have a girlfriend at all. Another source identified this mysterious lady as Rosa Dunn, but put her well outside Ingalls visiting her brother Bee, who was a part-time outlaw.

This pretty legend wouldn't die, and even produced some poetry, sloppy but sentimental. It's worth quoting in part:

> Shadows of dead men stand by the wall
> Watching the fun of the pioneer ball . . .
> Rose of the Cimarron, Bitter Creek's girl,
> Stood watching the dancers glide and whirl
> The dance grows wilder, they're young,
> don't you see:
> "Gosh," says Red Buck, "so were we."

It is odd that the author included Red Buck Weightman in this paean to love, for he was as vicious a killer as the West ever produced. Nevertheless, the Rose is permanently enshrined in the mythology of the West, partly under the auspices of Bill Tilghman, one of the truly outstanding lawmen of all time.

For Tilghman had a part in producing a film called *The Passing of the Oklahoma Outlaw*, and at each showing of the film, theatergoers could buy a little illustrated book retelling the film's story. And since the Rose was part of the myth, a photo was required.

And so the Rose of the Cimarron was duly shown, lovingly cradling a revolver. The photo was of a female convict—or, alternatively, a juvenile delinquent, loaned for the occasion and provided a revolver, presumably unloaded. The real Miss Dunn is said to have married a blacksmith and drifted off into obscurity, which probably pleased her.

But there were a few women who more closely fit the outlaw mold. Bonnie Parker was surely one of those; Bonnie was the real thing, a very tough cookie indeed, with no noticeable moral code except a fierce loyalty to Clyde Barrow, who was a pretty mangy sort even on his good days. It was a shame she hooked up with him, because Bonnie was a good deal smarter than Clyde and had some talent. Clyde had none, and wasn't very bright.

Bonnie caught the public fancy, as did some of the others. After all, a lady who roared about in an automobile brandishing a deadly weapon was a most uncommon thing, not to mention a lady photographed not only with the obligatory gun but with a cigar clutched between her teeth. Bonnie said it was all a joke and that all she really smoked were cigarettes, but the photo was a sensation.

Blanche Barrow, wife to Buck Barrow, Clyde's brother and partner in crime, was characterized as a sort of gun moll herself. She ran with her outlaw husband and Bonnie and Clyde until her husband was mortally wounded in a fight with the law at the Red Crown motor court in little Platte City, Missouri.

Blanche had little use for Clyde, whom she regarded as a murderous thug without much sense. She was probably right about everything, for Clyde was given to a long line of stupidities. At the Red Crown, for example, Clyde pinned newspapers up to keep out the unwelcome gaze of outsiders, even with the shades drawn. Blanche remarked, with some reason, that that "was enough to make anyone get suspicious."

She did some time for assault with intent to commit murder after the Platte City fight, although there is much reason to question whether she even fired a shot.

Her prison time did give her a chance to meet fellow inmate Edna Murray, known as the Kissing Bandit for her quaint history of kissing a victim she and her husband had robbed. Edna was not a violent robber herself, but she ran with several of them. And she was an accomplished escape artist as well, successfully running out on sentences three times. She managed to pass on some bad genes to her son, Preston Paden, who ended up in a Kansas prison for the murder of a night watchman.

There were a few other real molls. Vivian Chase was one, an active robber and kidnapper until she got herself murdered in 1935. And then there was Lillian Tackett, bank robber, who worked with her boyfriend until she got crossways with him and shot him down.

Still, most of those transmogrified by the press into "gun molls" were a flash in the pan, heap big smoke and no fire. They got a few days' headlines and then disappeared into oblivion. But a few acquired an undying fame; their deeds, mostly imaginary or vastly inflated, kept their image alive and glowing—and multiplying— through the years.

Belle Starr! Ah, now that's a name to conjure with! The outlaw queen, the fearless bandit leader, the heartthrob of my early youth. She was played on the silver screen by a lovely woman, Gene Tierney, about the time I had just discovered girls. I fell in love.

It wasn't until years later that I discovered it was all balderdash. The leading lady in the movie galloped about at the head of her outlaw band, adventurous and daring. She gave precise orders, and her outlaw minions obeyed her instantly and exactly. She wasn't all bad, of course; I forget why she turned outlaw, at least according to Hollywood.

I do recall that for all her galloping, I never saw her actually riding the horse; I suspect her saddle was on some sort of frame, and four or five strong men—below the camera's eye—created riding motions while the wind machine blew her hair about.

Imagine my chagrin when I later learned all about the real Belle and found out the legend was a cruel invention. Belle the daring, swashbuckling outlaw was a creation of many printed pages and many yards of film. Belle was written about at great length by an assortment of writers, some of whom even added to a wonderful myth.

Much overrated: Belle Starr.

The real Belle was born Myra Belle Shirley in Missouri, on a farm near the town of Carthage. Her father went from farming to inn-keeping and was accounted an affluent man for the time. Belle was accorded a privilege not enjoyed by most Missouri girls back then, attendance at the Carthage Female Academy, from which she graduated.

But then came the Civil War—the War Between the States, if you prefer—and her father lost much of what he had built. Add to that the loss of Belle's brother, Bud, killed while riding with a band of Missouri Bushwhackers.

There are all sorts of myths about Belle herself spying and scouting for the Bushwhackers, and one myth suggests that in that daring role she got to know Jesse James and Cole Younger. They were Bushwhackers, all right, but served with different bands. Anyhow, according to mythology, Belle was "fired to deeds of valor" by her "hot southern blood," overlooking the detail that Missouri was distinctly not the South but a much-contested border state.

Her father having lost much of his property as well as his son, the family moved down into Texas, settling near the town of Scyene, now part of Dallas. And there Belle, in the fresh bloom of youth, married a wanted criminal named Jim Reed. Two years into the marriage, the first child appeared, a daughter officially named Rosie. But Belle called the baby "her Pearl," and Pearl she remained for the rest of the daughter's days. For a while Belle and Reed lived down along the Canadian River on the property of Old Tom Starr, fearsome survivor of the bloody Cherokee internecine war.

And then, in 1871, they moved to California, where Reed went on with his profession, which at least by then was career criminal. There are stories that Belle helped him by working at fencing horses Reed stole. There are also tales of her doing some murdering and robbing herself, but the great probability is that those tales are just more of the "bandit queen" mythology.

Back in Oklahoma one particularly ugly offense committed by Reed was the brutalizing of one Watt Grayson, a wealthy Indian. When Grayson wouldn't tell Reed and his partners where his money was, they strung him up and let him strangle for a bit, then let him down and asked again. When Grayson refused them again, they turned on Grayson's wife and strung her up in the same way. At this Grayson told them what they wanted to know.

There is no more evidence that Belle was part of this monstrous act than evidence that she was part of the robbery of the Austin–San Antonio stagecoach, although Reed certainly was. And then in 1874 Reed took on a tough deputy sheriff in a gunfight and finished last, which was a good thing for everybody.

A vital part of the Belle Starr legend is that her Pearl was in fact the child of Cole Younger, although Cole denied paternity to the end of his days. Siring Pearl, the legend says, is why Tom Starr's place down near the Canadian was called Younger's Bend, a name given the area by Belle. But it wasn't. Old Tom himself gave his land the name; Tom, being a fur piece from sainthood himself, was just showing his admiration for a successful and well-known outlaw.

Being a widow now, Belle was officially free to shop around. She seems to have done so with enthusiasm, sampling the available wares, including a brief dalliance with Bruce Younger up in Kansas; a sub-myth says she married him, but if she did, the union did not last.

In time she did marry, this time Sam Starr, Old Tom's son. The happy couple settled in Younger's Bend, and things rolled along until 1883, when both Belle and Sam did a short term in the Detroit House of Corrections for horse theft. And then, about three years later, Sam attended a dance and ran into one Frank West, an old enemy. The inevitable followed, and the two shot each other into the next world; neither lasted more than a few minutes after the smoke blew away.

So Belle was single again.

What followed, if the stories are even half true, was a veritable smorgasbord of sexual delights with a whole batch of outlaws, men like Jim French, Jack Spaniard, and Jim July (who took the name of Jim Starr). The last man up seems to have been one Blue Duck, much younger than the now-aging Belle.

She didn't have the chance to grow much older, for Belle got crossways with a sharecropper on her land. He was called Ed Watson, and he turned out to be a wanted man, sought in Florida for a variety of crimes including murder. Belle discovered what he was and allegedly did not want to be accused of harboring a fugitive, so she told Watson to take a hike and returned his rent for the ground he was farming. And she is also supposed to have also told him that if he didn't go she knew that Florida officers would like to know where he was. That was a big mistake.

Shortly thereafter Belle was murdered from ambush, probably by Watson, but maybe even by her own son Ed—her second child by Reed—another suspect mentioned in the Belle Starr book of tall tales. Watson went back to Florida and killed some more people, and then met some lawmen who ushered him into the next world.

Ed Reed got full of hooch in 1896 and terrorized a saloon. To this irritation the saloon owner took umbrage, and that was the end of Reed. Belle's Pearl carried on with her profession, first as a prostitute and later as a madam. Surviving several arrests, she died in a hotel in Arizona in 1925.

Thus the deathless legend of Belle Starr.

Cora Hubbard has been characterized as a second Belle Starr, although she was mostly lawless with her mouth. With two punks of equally limited intelligence, she embarked on a career of robbery in 1897. The trio chose a bank in Pineville, Missouri; Cora held the horses while the two men entered the bank.

They got a few dollars but had no workable plan for escape, and all three were soon swept up by the law. Cora was found in possession of a .45 Colt with "Bob Dalton" inscribed on the butt and seven notches cut in it. Cora had boasted before that she'd run with the Dalton Gang, and that seemed to be some sort of proof that her claim might even be true. Trouble is, there is no Cora Hubbard anyplace in the history of the Daltons.

In any case, Cora got twelve years for this dinky robbery and didn't get out until 1905. Femme fatale she surely wasn't, one reporter commenting on her "greasy dark complexion." Somebody also compared her to Kate Bender, of the vile Bender family who murdered at least eight people back in the 1870s. That was hardly very flattering, but maybe in Cora's eyes it beat a greasy dark complexion. So much for being an outlaw legend.

But if the Belle and Cora myths are 90 percent phony, Pearl Hart's saga was not, even if she too is surrounded by some fanciful legends. Her career as an outlaw was short but spectacular, at least for a diminutive woman.

Pearl was Canadian by birth and ran away from home at about sixteen. She married a man named Hart, who can be fairly described as the lowest form of life. They settled in Arizona, and Pearl had a child by him, but their married life thereafter was sporadic at best. Pearl had a second child, although the story goes that the second baby's paternity was questionable.

Hart beat on Pearl from time to time, which was bad. Almost worse, he was shiftless, perennially allergic to honest toil. Pearl gave him the gate at least three times, until the rift was permanent. In the intervals between bouts with Hart, and after his final departure, Pearl supported herself any way she could. She may have been a camp cook, a prostitute, or a singer, or maybe all of these. She "wrestled with the world," as one newspaper put it, "in a catch-as-catch-can style."

In time Pearl was faced with a crisis at home, in the form of a letter telling her that her mother was very ill back in Canada; the news, as she put it, "drove me crazy." Pearl didn't have money enough for train fare home, and that, she later told a jury, was the only reason she turned to crime.

The invitation to go bad probably came from an outlaw called Joe Boot, although Pearl later wrote in *Cosmopolitan* magazine that she gave the orders and Joe had to follow them, "or I would have killed him, and he knew it too," a sensational revelation very probably invented for publication. Talking to a jury later, all contrition, she said she had only agreed to violate the law if Joe would promise that nobody would be hurt.

Whoever said what when to whom, the pair embarked on a dirty game as old as mankind. Pearl would attract a man who

Pearl Hart.

looked like he had at least some money. She would then lure him to her room and entertain him, if that's the word, until Boot entered, knocked the sucker around, and robbed him. For some reason Pearl and her co-conspirator were dissatisfied with the results of this violent scheme. Whether it was a shortage of loot or too much interest from the law or an angry dupe with a pistol is unknown. Or, an alternative tale tells that the pair ran a brothel.

Whatever it was they did, it didn't work, or it didn't work fast enough, and so they turned to robbery. It was to be a stagecoach, just like the big boys. They chose a spot at a curve where they knew the stage to Globe would have to slow down. And there they successfully stopped the coach, stuck up the driver and passengers, and made off with something between four hundred and five hundred dollars. One account of the robbery states that as smoothly as it seemed to go, the driver recognized both of the robbers.

Pearl graciously gave each of the passengers back a buck so they could buy something to eat. In addition to the money they got, Pearl also found two pistols shoved down in the seat cushion of the coach and appropriated those, too. She would come to wish she hadn't.

Now it was time for the retreat, and here is where things began to go badly wrong. In typical amateur fashion Pearl and Joe hadn't done much by way of planning their escape. The idea was to ride to the town of Benson, there to catch a train and disappear. But they obviously had not planned their escape very well.

They traveled over very rough country at night, lying up during daylight, spending one full day in a cave and another camped elsewhere when they should have been riding for their lives. They obviously had no sense of urgency, in spite of knowing there would be posses combing the countryside for them.

Along the way Joe managed to fall into a creek, horse and all. Pearl wrote later that he "went down twice," requiring Pearl to fish him out and pump water out of him. The escape was not going well.

And at last they found themselves hopelessly lost. That dismal reality must have occurred to them when they emerged again on the stage road, not far from where they had held up the stagecoach in the first place. Exhausted, with very tired horses, they camped for the night, making their dinner of cold beans.

The dinner was lousy, the night was uncomfortable, but the next morning was infinitely worse. They awoke looking into a couple of rifle muzzles owned by members of a sheriff's posse. Their experiment in crime was over for all time.

All that remained was the trial. Just figuring out how to lodge Pearl in jail was a knotty problem, which spoke volumes about the rarity of a female felon. Pearl seems to have swapped her rough duds for more ladylike garb, moving the *Phoenix Republican* to unkindly and somewhat mysteriously comment that she "proved not as good-looking a girl as she had been as a boy," which, to judge from Pearl's picture, is not entirely believable.

Nevertheless, in due course proper accommodations were found for Pearl. She broke out of jail once, just like the career felons, but tough lawman George Scarborough caught her and she was returned for trial. Pearl testified on her own behalf, and she did a masterful job of it. She turned on the tears and invoked the spirit of her mother wasting away because her daughter could not come to help her. She did so well at tugging on heartstrings, in fact, that against all the evidence the jury found her not guilty.

Pearl was of course ecstatic. How Joe felt is not recorded, since he had already been sentenced to a heavy-duty sentence (he did not serve most of it, escaping to disappear from history). And Pearl's ecstasy was short-lived, because the law, unhappy with the jury's verdict, remembered the two pistols she had stolen from the coach, charged her with those larcenies before a different jury, and this time got a conviction and a five-year sentence.

And so Pearl went off to Yuma, the hellhole of anybody's penal system, and there the administration went through the usual difficulty in figuring out how to house their only woman. She was pardoned after serving about half her sentence, and even then mythology surrounded her departure from Yuma.

One story says she claimed she was pregnant and thereby secured her release. It was especially easy, the story goes, because she had been alone only with a trusty, a minister of the gospel, and, of all people, the governor of the Arizona Territory. The potential for governmental embarrassment being obviously quite high, Pearl was a free woman. Well, maybe it happened that way, but at best it was no more than half true, because our Pearl, as it turned out, was obviously not pregnant. The whole reason-for-pardon yarn seems to be somebody's invention, but it's just too good to leave out.

Pearl's later history is uncertain. She may have been part of a Wild West show, or a pickpocket, or maybe she ran a cigar store. The most likely end for Pearl was pretty prosaic, a long career in Dripping Springs, Arizona, as a rancher's wife. You kind of hope so.

Most outlaws had some "ladies" who accompanied them, but few seem to have been more than camp followers. A couple of youngsters called Little Britches and Cattle Annie graced—if that's the word—the camp of the Doolin gang and posed for photos carrying weaponry, but it is not recorded that they ever fired a shot in anger.

The legends of the Dalton Gang also include a supposed outlaw called Flo Quick, maybe the same woman as a real horse thief calling herself Tom King. Tom seems to have been a real outlaw who disappeared into the misty realm of legend—she either married or formed her own gang and was killed during a holdup gone bad in Wichita, or maybe it was Tombstone. It depends on what account you read.

Or maybe Flo was really Eugenia Moore, who may have been the mysterious lady who had her photo taken with Bob Dalton not long before he ended up dead at Coffeyville. But either one of them may have been somebody named Daisy Bryant, reputed to be Bob's bedfellow. Or not.

Eugenia is supposed to have been the intelligence arm of the gang, seducing express agents for information on valuable train shipments or simply flirting with them while she listened to the clatter of the telegraph (oh, yes, she was also an accomplished telegraphist).

The 1920s and '30s produced some real gun molls, as the twentieth-century journalists were fond of calling outlaws' female companions. A couple of them are worth mentioning.

One was Margaret Collins, who came to Chicago from New York in 1924, after her gangster lover had been extinguished by a rival's bullet. Next stop was local hoodlum Johnny Sheehy. Their flaming romance was abruptly terminated when Sheehy expired of a lawman's bullet. All poor Johnny did was pull his own gun and kill two restaurant workers because they wouldn't bring Margaret a bowl of ice cubes; she only wanted to throw them at the band.

Margaret didn't mourn overlong, taking up with one Phillips, another thug, who departed this life when he knocked around a singer in a nightclub and the police intervened. Margaret moved on to somebody called Jew Bates, until Bates had to leave town in a hurry. In 1930 Bates shuffled off this mortal coil down in Kentucky, where he had taken up residence as a bootlegger.

Long before his death Margaret had taken up with another criminal, another nobody called Schlig, who showered Margaret with diamonds until he ended up dead. The man who allegedly filled him full of bullets acquired Margaret, too, at least until he too was murdered. Margaret passed on to Sam Katz, a robber, who made the mistake of taking on Chicago's finest. He lost.

Margaret left town for a while after that, did a little shoplifting and did a little time, before she returned to Chicago and took up with yet another gangster, a hood named Feldman. Feldman survived a wound from a police bullet, but collapsed during a court session and departed this life abruptly.

It served him right. The wound from the cop's bullet had broken open when he waxed angry at Margaret for dancing too close with another man and broke a bottle over her head. The resulting restraint by several other male patrons left Feldman much damaged, with several broken ribs.

The palmy days were over for Margaret, She survived the humiliation of a vagrancy arrest and another for stealing fur coats and yet another apparently for being present in a "dope house." She dropped from sight in the early 1940s, after two decades in the fast lane.

Florence Diggs had some time in the same fast lane, too. She married one Tim Murphy, a union thug with a sideline in robbery and other crime; they lived happily together until some other criminals filled him full of tommy gun slugs. Ten months later his sorrowing widow married one of his pallbearers, John Oberta, aka Dingbat. She became a widow again when Dingbat died of bullet sickness.

That was a real heartbreaker for poor Florence, who complained bitterly that she had been married to "two of the swellest guys that ever lived, and both get bumped off." If those two hoods were among the swellest fellers she knew, what on earth must her other male acquaintances have been like?

These are just a few of the molls who grace the history of American robbery.

Eleanor Jarman, dubbed the Blond Tigress by the papers, was one of the few serious female criminals of the '30s. She and the punks she ran with—George Dale and Leo Minneci—had pulled at least forty-eight robberies, during which Eleanor had amused herself by bashing victims, storekeepers and the like, with her blackjack. The papers said she was the leader of the pack, the "brains of the three."

If she was indeed the brains, the rest of them must have been cretins, for nothing the three did worked out right for them. The trio ended up murdering a haberdasher. George Dale got a date with the electric chair for that one, while Eleanor and Leo had to be content with a mere 199 years.

More successful was Juanita Spinelli, called the Duchess. She actually made the big time—the gas chamber—for a series of felonies, including murder. And Stella Irwin—Sure-Shot Stella in the press—had a brief career shooting at pursuing police cars while her bank-robber boyfriend drove the getaway car.

But really active criminal ladies were not that common. Some were creations of the press, like Ma Barker, the "mastermind" of the Barker gang, who couldn't, said one gang member, organize a meal. Lillian Tackett was a real bank robber, and Dorcas Bancan (nom de crime Sally Scott) had a short run as a holdup girl. She was called the Godless Girl for a fairly bland tattoo she wore, not something you saw among the ladies every day back then.

Blanche Barrow ran with Bonnie and Clyde, sticking with her husband, Clyde's brother Buck. She did some time for her criminal career, but as far as anybody knows, she didn't shoot anybody.

But she did write a book.

Chapter 11

THE LAWMEN

THE HISTORY OF THE WEST is full of the exploits of some of the toughest outlaws ever bred. That history would have been far bloodier, far grimmer for the ordinary man and woman, had it not been for that extraordinary breed of man, the frontier lawman. They were called by various titles, marshal and sheriff and constable among them, but the best of them shared a couple of virtues.

First, they weren't afraid of much of anything. They couldn't be. The men they dealt with ranged from simple drunks to the worst of professional killers. You could get shot on the street or in the corner saloon, from ambush, or even in your home or at church. You couldn't count on anything, as witness what happened to lawman Billy Wilson.

Wilson—that wasn't his real name—started out on the wrong side of the law. For a time he was a part of the New Mexico trash that followed Billy the Kid. When Pat Garrett broke up the Kid's gang and killed its leader, Wilson survived, escaped from custody, and disappeared. He proved to be the unusual outlaw—he ultimately married, started a family, and went straight.

Years later Pat Garrett went to bat for Wilson—living under the alias David Anderson, his birth name—and got him a full pardon. The ex-bandit ended up a lawman, first a customs agent and then sheriff of Terrell County, Texas.

Even as wary a man as Wilson relaxed too far when he went out to make a routine arrest of a cowboy named Ed Valentine, who had gotten himself far too full of tarantula juice at a saloon in Sanderson, Texas. Valentine was engaged in raising hell at the railroad station. Wilson knew the man and expected no trouble, but when he tried to arrest Valentine, the cowboy ducked into a baggage shed, or maybe it was a stable, depending on which account you read.

When Wilson followed him, Valentine shot the lawman without warning from the darkness inside the building. Valentine was killed by another officer—or maybe he died of angry mob disease, Wilson being a popular officer in town—but Wilson couldn't be saved.

If officers had to be bold, they also had to be very good with the shootin' iron of their choice. The lawman commonly chose a shotgun when he could, a big one, ten- or twelve-gauge, which at close range would throw a lot of buckshot or a slug. If you hit your adversary right, you could practically cut him in half, and since there was no choke on the cannons, you had every chance of disabling him. Then there was the intimidation factor: Staring down a bore that big encouraged prompt obedience. In the words of a robbery victim, the barrel of the holdup man's weapon looked "big enough to sleep in," or as another said, "as big as a hat."

There were rare exceptions, like Bear River Tom Smith, who seldom carried a gun and relied on a pair of very hard fists and pure daring to cow his opposition. He was finally killed by a pair of outlaws while marshal of roaring Abilene, Kansas.

If the lawman thought he might meet trouble at a somewhat longer range, the rifle was his choice, ordinarily Mr. Winchester's dependable lever-action. And most everybody carried a revolver, generally the reliable Colt, although the Hollywood *stalk-down-the-street-cuss-out-your-opponent-and-rely-on-a-draw-of-blinding-speed* nonsense was rare as hen's teeth. It wasn't the first shot that mattered; it was, as Wyatt Earp cogently commented, the first *aimed* round.

There were disabilities, too, besides the constant danger. Pay was always uniformly lousy, even for federal officers, and you normally provided your own horses, weapons, and ammunition. You paid your own possemen, too, and hoped that a penurious government would reimburse you . . . sometime. It was a little like being a knight without armor and working for Ebeneezer Scrooge. And if you stopped a bullet, there was no such thing as a pension to keep your family from starving.

A lot of the toughest of the lawmen were deputy U.S. marshals, legendary figures like the Three Guardsmen, Heck Thomas, Bill Tilghman, and Chris Madsen, who rode for Judge Isaac Parker's court out of Fort Smith, Arkansas. They and their companions rode into the wild country of Indian Territory, out across the Arkansas River, where some sixty deputy marshals were murdered during Judge Parker's tenure.

Another very tough, capable deputy marshal was Frank Dalton, brother to the famous—if overrated—Dalton Boys, who ended up very dead in Coffeyville, Kansas. Frank was killed down in the brakes of the Arkansas, trying to make an arrest. Another officer with him killed two of his murderers; a third was run down by another marshal later. That was the way of it, life not only out in Indian Territory but elsewhere on the advancing frontier.

They were a colorful lot. Big Bass Reeves, an ex-slave, managed to survive in the wild country west across the Arkansas and killed several outlaws in the process of enforcing the law. He also had his spiritual side, evident when he chained his prisoners securely to the wagon at night and proceeded to preach to them at length, mostly about the danger into which they risked their immortal souls.

And if that didn't scare the criminals into worrying about their spiritual future, there was more soul saving for the sentenced outlaws from Judge Parker, whose lecture, said one outlaw, was almost as hard to hear as the actual sentence.

These men and their comrades were remarkable enough, but the most remarkable lawman of all time was probably a man very few people have ever heard of, Deputy U.S. Marshal Joseph Wiley

Evans. He was very tough, and courageous to a fault, but so were a lot of other lawmen in the West. Evans was special for another reason: He had only one arm.

One source tells that in his time Evans ran down more outlaws than anybody else in early Arizona—that was before the heyday of the Earps and Texas John Slaughter, to be sure, but it's still a phenomenal record, especially for a man with the kind of burden Evans had to carry.

One story about him gives a clear picture of the man. Back in the spring of 1877, the stage to Ehrenberg was stopped just west of the town of Wickenberg by two bandits, Brophy and Sutton. There was a lawman on board, but he was engaged in transporting an insane woman to a California asylum and could not resist.

The bandits got away, but got to the crossing of the Colorado River too late to cross into California. They became nervous during the wait, however, and decided to leave town. Sutton went to collect their horses and gear, while Brophy watched their back trail from a spot in front of Mill's Saloon.

They didn't make it, for their descriptions had preceded them. Before Sutton could return, Evans and one Colonel Bryan approached Brophy and a movie-style point-blank shoot-out followed. Bryan's shotgun turned out to be loaded with birdshot instead of something heavier—plan ahead—and only wounded the outlaw. It was up to Evans.

In spite of blood flooding into his eyes from a head wound, Evans shot Brophy down, and then as Sutton appeared and opened up with a Henry rifle, sixteen cartridges of firepower, Evans held his ground with Bryan and shot it out with the outlaw.

It was an epic fight, fifteen minutes and an estimated sixty shots, but it ended simply when Sutton decided it wasn't worth it and surrendered. While the story of the fight doesn't say much for the marksmanship of anybody concerned, it speaks volumes for the courage of them all, especially tough Joe Evans, who had to shoot and reload his revolver with one hand.

Evans went on to a long career in the service of the law. He had already captured the first stage robbers in Arizona and went on, as one story says, to have a dozen "post office rewards" pending at once. And he is said to be the man who told Wyatt Earp that Frank Stillwell was laying an ambush for him in Tucson. It is pleasant to relate that he ended his long career at a peaceful civilian desk.

But of all the tough lawmen who walked the West, the man who was probably most lethal was the man who finally cleaned up Cochise County, Arizona, after the Earp boys and Doc Holliday had left Tombstone. He was a successful rancher, who had driven big herds up from Texas and built himself an empire on a huge spread down in the San Simon Valley of southern Arizona.

His name was John Slaughter, called Texas John naturally, and he was by nature a man of peace, a good family man who loved children and hated any kind of cruelty to animals. But Slaughter had a very direct and elementary view of the world of humans: There were two kinds of people, he thought, good and bad. The good people you protected; the bad ones you killed or ran out of the country. Simple.

Cattle rustlers who cast covetous eyes on Slaughter's herds generally ended up permanently dead, for according to Slaughter's philosophy, formal trials of bad people were unimportant and due process even less so. Even the fierce Apache, wonderfully efficient cattle thieves, eventually left Texas John's herds alone. They recognized another warrior when they saw one.

It was inevitable that the good folks would also recognize him as just the hombre to lead the forces of law and order. And so, after the Earps had departed Tombstone, Slaughter became sheriff of Arizona's Cochise County. If the Earps and their followers had disposed of some of the trash, there was a lot left.

There was a lot less of it when John Slaughter was finished. He was famous for trailing stock thieves, as a rule returning with the stock but without the thieves. Consistent with his philosophy, the stock belonged to somebody honest; the thieves were clearly bad people.

JOHN H. SLAUGHTER,

Deadly: Texas John Slaughter.

Slaughter didn't talk much, but every word meant something. Take, for example, his advice to his deputies, prefaced by his usual opening words: "I say, I say, shoot first and shout 'Throw up your hands' after." It saved a lot of trouble.

So did his procedure with lesser criminals. Once a man was identified as a running sore on the behind of civilization, Slaughter would visit him and issue some clear advice: You have a week (three days) (twenty-four hours) to be out of Cochise County. If the object of his attention turned defiant, or asked why, Slaughter simply said that the alternative to leaving was dealing with him.

Slaughter's suggestion was generally enough.

The "law dogs," as some called them, mostly lived on, their lives less complicated after the permanent departure of the famous criminals they had hunted for so long.

Famous lawmen like Tom Smith, Bat and Ed Masterson, Bill Tilghman, and Heck Thomas have won a well-deserved share of the law-enforcement fame of the early West. It's an honor they share with other famous names: the Earps, Jeff Milton, George Scarborough, Pat Garrett, Burt Mossman, and the Sugrue brothers.

Lawmen in the first decades of the twentieth century were equally tough. Grover Bishop, long-time lawman and two-term sheriff of wild Cherokee County, finished his career with a total of fourteen dead badmen to his credit, some sort of record even among the lawmen of the day, men with a similarly low tolerance for killers and robbers.

He favored the Thompson submachine gun, which went a long way toward evening the odds in firepower. "If I hadn't used one," he said, "I wouldn't have lasted as long as a snowball in you know where." The story goes that he also carried a matched pair of semiautomatic Luger pistols.

Grover minced no words concerning the men he was charged with bringing to justice. He would, he said, offer his quarry the chance to "go in like a man." If the bad man didn't like that idea, the alternative was "I'm gonna shoot you and drag you in." That seemed plain enough, and he meant it. On at least one occasion, he hauled two dead outlaws into town, part of them hanging out of his trunk and trailing blood. He finished by dumping the remains unceremoniously at the local undertaker's door, and there they stayed for a while, for the edification of the populace.

Depending on which side you favored, you either hated him or thought he was the finest cop ever spawned, the honest man's friend and protector. At least nobody was ambivalent about Grover. There is more about the formidable Bishop in chapter 15 ("Thug"), the history of the so-called Tri-State Terror, Wilber Underhill, and some of the other Cookson Hills outlaws.

Grover is not to be confused with Luther Bishop, one of only three agents staffing the infant Oklahoma Bureau of Criminal Identification and Investigation. Luther was an equally tough lawman, who is credited with, among other virtuous deeds, exterminating long-time pest Al Spencer (see chapter 9). And Luther was one of the officers who helped solve the series of murders up in the Osage, a deliberate campaign of murdering Indians to get control of their oil interests in that petroleum-rich area.

Nor were people uncertain about Mark Lairmore, who'd been instrumental in bringing Underhill to justice and helped out with the capture of the poisonous Eno boys. He was a veteran of a good many shooting scrapes, including one in which he took on three punks and shot and wounded all of them. He finished his earthly race with a score of nine—he was wounded himself on three occasions—and was not only head instructor in marksmanship for the Tulsa Police but a prolific writer on the gentle science of gunfighting.

They don't make 'em like that these days.

Chapter 12

"BUY MORE BULLETS"

The Citizens Fight Back

UP IN BACKWATERS LIKE THE Cookson Hills of eastern
Oklahoma, and in a few other places, outlaws could count on some
help from some of the people living there, or at least a tolerance, a
silence that was almost as good. But in most of the country, even in
the bowels of the Great Depression, a robber or killer was considered the lowest form of life. And when the chance came to deal with
outlaws, alone or helping their local lawman, there was no shortage
of volunteers who laid their lives on the line for their towns.

In this modern day of "I don't want to get involved," that's
hard for a lot of people to understand. In celebrated cases from
long ago, like the Dalton Boys in Coffeyville, Kansas, or the James-
Younger Gang in Northfield, Minnesota, it's easy to say well, gee,
that was the Wild West, as if that explained the difference in the
courage and initiative of the population.

But there is and was a great deal more to it. These people
who rose up and took on hardened criminals were ordinary folks,
farmers and small business owners, and they did it out of pride in
themselves and their little towns and a stubborn refusal to let outlaw punks push them around. The Daltons and the James boys get

their own space in this book, but there are lots of other notable examples of civic defiance.

There was Cisco, Texas, of a December day in 1927. Into town, with their greedy eyes fixed firmly on the little town's bank, drove four of the stupidest criminals in all the annals of American crime, which is saying quite a lot. They were led by a moron named Marshall Ratliff, who for some obscure reason entered Cisco clad as Santa Claus and left his car-borne confederates to walk several blocks to the bank—to the delight of passing children.

Ratliff and two of his little elves were all ex-cons, beneficiaries of one Miriam "Ma" Ferguson, governor of Texas and a weird bird indeed. Ma made a habit of releasing felons from the state's prisons, on the average of something like a hundred each month, as charges of corruption and bribery orbited around her like vultures.

Ratliff's brother, also an ex-con, was supposed to go along on the bank raid, but he managed to get himself arrested, again, and so was unavailable. His substitute, named Davis, was added at the last minute.

The holdup was bungled, although the robbers were armed to the teeth; at least two of them were carrying not one but two handguns. At first it went well—they got some money—but then a mother and daughter walked in, saw what was happening, and marched right out another door. Another customer looked through the bank window and shouted that the bank was being robbed. One of the robbers fired at him without success—and if the robbers didn't know before now that they were in trouble, they did when a shot was fired in return *at* the bank from outside.

The mother got hold of somebody at city hall, and Chief of Police Bit Bedford set out for the bank with a shotgun and some help. Much of the town was scrambling for guns and making for the bank as well. The outlaws finally realized it was high time to get out of Cisco, and so they made for the alley where their car awaited, herding a small crowd of hostages, both bank employees and customers.

In the alley they ran into a bombardment from several directions, and the crowd of hostages seized the moment and ran away. A couple of them were wounded, but that didn't stop them and it sure didn't help Ratliff and his little band of blunderers. Another hostage was forced into the car, but slid deftly clear across the seat to the other door and just kept going. In no time flat the robbers were left with only two hostages, a pair of little girls.

The officers had arrived, but they were handicapped by trying to engage the enemy but still protect the hostages. One deputy was shot in the head and Sheriff Bedford went down with five wounds— a citizen picked up his gun and emptied it at the criminals. And Bedford had gotten a round into one of the bandits besides Ratliff, who was already hit and limping badly. The bandits hastily climbed into their car and fled.

Not far. Not only was one tire flat from a bullet, but they suddenly discovered that the gas gauge read almost empty. It was a triumph of planning; they had forgotten to top up the tank. Nevertheless, they kept up their flight for a little way, with one outlaw firing at the pursuit from a smashed-out rear window. But at last it dawned on even them that they'd better do something fast or their great holdup was over.

What to do? Why, steal another car, of course. And so they stopped a family named Harris and hijacked their car. Or thought they did. They transferred their loot to the new wheels while one gang member—Robert Hill—filled the air with bullets, trying to hold up the pursuit. They also loaded up gang member Louis Davis, who was badly shot up, and then everybody hopped in.

Away they should have gone at high speed. They would have, too, except that the driver of the Harris car—fourteen-year-old Woody—had thoughtfully removed the keys. Curses, foiled again!

So it was back to their old, almost gasless car, and in their panicked flight they managed to forget the badly wounded Davis. They got down the road a ways and then it also occurred to them they'd forgotten their loot as well, some twelve thousand dollars in cash plus some securities. "Oh, hell!" quoth one of the bandits, which pretty well summed up their day so far, but there was no going back with a whole angry town coming after you.

They tried to elude the pursuit by swinging off the main road, but succeeded only in getting their car stuck. At this point they abandoned their little hostages and ran for it, as fast as you can with two of your number seriously shot up. Now every man's hand was against them, particularly when popular Sheriff Bedford died; the wounded deputy was dying, too, and several of the citizen hostages were also wounded.

The outlaws now stole another car, which they managed to wreck on, of all things, a cattle guard. Appealing to a farmer's better instincts, they got another car with the farmer's son to drive. They drove around all one day and then hid out for a night. The next morning they stole still another car and let their young driver go; it is not known just where the outlaws thought they were, but when their young hostage got to an inhabited area, he found out that he was back in . . . Cisco.

They were now being chased by several posses and lawmen from all over the place, not to mention the Texas Rangers, including the very deadly Sergeant "Lone Wolf" Gonzaullas. Ratliff, spotted by a posse, simply couldn't run anymore because of his leg wound. So he went into the bag, and so did his astonishing arsenal: six automatic pistols, three pistol belts of ammo, a shotgun, and, to top it all off, a Bowie knife.

The other two robbers lasted a little longer but were finally arrested in Graham, Texas. They had seven bullet wounds apiece. When they were arrested, one man tried to escape but could only stagger. The other just leaned against a wall and then fell down. In time, one of them got a long prison term; the other was proved to have killed both police officers in Cisco, and he got a short acquaintanceship with the electric chair.

Ratliff, also on death row, managed a very successful insanity act in Huntsville prison, and the people of Cisco began to realize he might escape punishment entirely. So a local judge issued a bench warrant for him for theft of the Harris automobile. Back at the scene of the trial, Ratliff went into his crazy act again, and so lulled his jailers into thinking he really wasn't running on all eight. It got him out of his cell; once out, Ratliff got hold of a gun and killed one jailer.

But it didn't get him out of jail, because the head jailer took the pistol away from him and beat him half to death with it. The citizenry finished the job, in the form of a mob that may have numbered a thousand. Dragging Santa Claus out of the jail, they hung him . . . twice. The knot didn't stay tied the first time—or maybe, according to one version of the tale, the rope broke. But the second try was successful.

All of which brings us to the battle of Mill Creek, up in Oklahoma. This little Johnston County town was a quiet place ordinarily. Most of the crime was penny-ante stuff: indecent exposure, bootlegging, the usual drunks, and a couple of more intriguing offenses, like dynamiting fish and something called "disturbing religious worship."

But there were also the occasional felonies, like the 1910 explosion in Wapanucka, where somebody tried to blow up the bank vault. They failed and ended up in a gun battle with a doughty town constable. When he ran out of ammunition and ran to get more, the would-be robbers fled on, of all things, a railroad handcar, pumping madly off into the night.

Then there was the Bromide bank robbery in 1919, and the Mill Creek bank was attacked in 1927 and again in 1931. In the 1931 raid the bank employees hid out in the vault, leaving the robbers to ransack the cash drawers. Those robbers were caught, and after escaping once from the Johnston County lockup, they were duly tried and sent up for ten years.

But the really violent attack came in 1932, when on a cool, cloudy March afternoon, three robbers drove up to the bank. What the bandits didn't know was that things had changed in Mill Creek. It was the heart of the Depression, the FDIC had not appeared yet, and the bank had been told that if it was robbed again it might lose its private deposit insurance. That would have been a catastrophe for the little farm town, because the bank would have to close.

So the residents made ready for anything. The bank had bought an alarm, which was silent inside the building but rang in several neighboring businesses. The merchants downtown had formed a home guard, which they more formally called the "planned bank robbery watch," and they kept their weapons by them.

And so, when Luther Smalley and Fred Hamner strolled into the bank and demanded all that money, their own little Armageddon was awaiting them. Outside in the getaway car waited Adam Richetti, who would go on to greater things, running for a time with Pretty Boy Floyd and becoming an outlaw star when he became part of the Kansas City massacre and went to the electric chair as a consequence.

The robbers had intended to take the bankers with them as hostages, but the bankers had wisely taken refuge in the vault, and so the robbers walked into the street without hostages.

When Smalley and Hamner left the bank, carrying some eight hundred dollars of the citizens' money, about a dozen men of the home guard opened up on them, and their shooting was phenomenal. The top of Hamner's head was "shot clean off," as a Mill Creek resident put it, whereof he immediately expired. Smalley was hit repeatedly and ended up on the pavement in front of the bank in a puddle of his own blood, trying to crawl toward his dropped weapon. The bank's cashier kicked it away from him.

Richetti stuck a rifle through the car window and returned the fire, hitting nothing but a spectator's hat, until it dawned on him that it was time to go. The car already resembled a sieve, and he had been hit several times. And so he roared off down the street and promptly took a wrong turn down a farm road.

He capped his dismal driving performance by getting the car bogged down, no doubt helped by a flat tire, the result of the citizens' accurate fire. There were twenty-eight holes from bullets or buckshot in the car, the result of only seventeen shots fired by the home guard, and that didn't count the holes in the outlaws.

The pursuing citizens followed a blood trail from the car into a grove of trees, and there was Richetti, not nearly so tough any more. He had taken a rifle bullet in one leg and was spattered here and there with buckshot. He was captured without resistance.

The superintendent of schools called an assembly and then took everybody downtown to view the blood-spattered street in front of the bank, decorated with some of Hamner's few brains. The superintendent completed his edifying "Crime does not pay" outing with a trip to an abandoned building, where Hamner's remains had been summarily dumped. A few of the kids were a little queasy by then and opted out of the Hamner viewing, but most felt as a Mill Creek resident did; as she said to the author, "We wouldn't have missed it for the world."

The Oklahoma Bankers Association paid a reward to the home guard for Hamner, five hundred dollars, which was a good deal of money back then. The reward for the other two, on their way to prison, was only one hundred dollars apiece, they being still alive. Obviously and understandably, Oklahoma bankers had had quite enough of bank robbers, for the Sooner State had become the happy hunting ground for them. It was better that such criminals be permanently erased, for the good of the banking business and citizens in general.

For a while there was some threat of vengeance for the demise of the robbers, mostly in anonymous letters, but that ceased over time. One lowlife who said something approaching a threat in town was summarily invited to "get your ass out of Mill Creek," advice that he took.

The *Daily Oklahoman*, then as now the state's leading newspaper, waxed positively eloquent over the victory of the home guard. Some of their highfalutin praise is worth repeating:

> They became William Tells of the shotgun. They could uncap the sheriff's confiscated beer bottles at fifty paces.

When asked what they would do with the bounty paid for the bandits, extinct and otherwise, they announced that they would "buy more bullets."

Smalley didn't make it out of prison, being murdered by other inmates, and Richetti was on his way to execution. As the Bankers Association piously commented about everybody's favorite, jocular good ol' boy Charles Arthur Floyd, better known to the public as Pretty Boy, "He will take his place with the others in the silent city of the dead."

And he did.

Floyd had left Oklahoma for fresh adventures in robbery and never returned, except to attend a huge funeral out in the Cookson Hills—his own. Maybe he left in part because he missed his right hand, mercurial nitwit George Birdwell, who had made the terminal error of trying to rob the bank in Boley.

Floyd and Birdwell had done a lot of bank robbing, including the bank of Morris, Oklahoma, not once but twice. Pretty Boy was much given to joking with the helpless customers and employees during his robberies; no doubt it amused him to act the comic for a literally captive audience, joking in the Morris bank that he and his partner were "back for a return engagement." It is not recorded that his audience was much amused, although the local paper reported that the bank had been revisited by the "Same Pair of Jovial Bank Robbers."

The raids were only a couple of months apart, the second one just before Christmas. The second raid produced a reaction very like that in Mill Creek—the formation of a citizens' defense committee. They chose firing positions and the bank got itself a silent alarm.

And sure enough, it happened, the third invasion in eight months. This time it wasn't Floyd, who was probably too smart to risk still another return engagement. This time, in May 1932, the invaders were three: Roscoe Ernest, called Red, Troy Kittrell, and another man who remains unidentified.

The job seemed like a pushover. Only young teller Clara Aggas was on duty in the bank, and she could do nothing to impede Ernest and the third man, who came into the bank without masks and waving handguns. Clara was all cooperation in hauling money out of

Heroine Clara Aggas.

MR. HERMAN THOMPSON AND MS. NINA WALKER

the vault; or she seemed to be, for she fired the alarm from a button in the vault. She made a great show out of carrying money from the vault but dragged out the process as long as she dared.

The bandits thought Clara would make a fine shield, and so they dragged her along when they went outside to get in their car. The home guard and the town marshal were waiting. The getaway driver, Red Ernest, saw the marshal and opened fire, slightly wounding him. The owner of the hardware store replied with his .30-.30 from a second-story window and nailed Ernest in the head. The outlaw slumped over the wheel in a pool of blood, dead or dying.

Now the two inside men made for the car, and most of the citizens had to hold their fire for fear of hitting Clara. The unidentified robber was hit at least once, but he and Kittrell made the vehicle, pulling Red Ernest from behind the wheel and finally driving away with Clara and their wounded cohort. Somewhere in all of this, Clara was badly wounded, and the presence of powder burns on her face showed that she had been shot by one of the bandits, probably Kittrell.

And so, with the townsmen still holding their fire, the bandits drove out of Morris a couple of miles and then turned off on a dirt road where they had stashed another car. They resumed their flight, callously abandoning Clara and the remains of Ernest. But Clara, badly hurt and covered with blood, managed to crawl to the main road, where she was found by Barron Skinner, who just happened to be her future husband. He rushed her to the hospital in Okmulgee.

Ernest was quickly identified as a "wandering evangelist and small-time thief," a curious combination of occupations. He was also wanted for some robberies in another county.

Clara, meanwhile, was being treated in Okmulgee and being lionized by the town newspaper as "plucky" and beautiful. She was certainly both. She would ultimately spend a substantial time in Philadelphia, undergoing plastic surgery to rebuild her chin, a procedure then in its infancy.

Kittrell, Oklahoma-born, was run down somewhat later, in Detroit, of all places. He sang to the police, a somewhat confused apologia built around the idea that he'd been forced into the bank robbery as well as an earlier holdup by Ernest, who was conveniently dead. The court was not impressed by this "poor me" performance and sent Kittrell up for twenty-five years.

Nobody ever recovered the bank's money nor proved the identity of the third man, who may have gotten in Kittrell's way, or was worse hit than it first appeared, and ended up dead someplace. It is pleasant to relate that Clara married her rescuer Barron as they had planned and produced a large family. She died at the ripe age of eighty-eight and lived to see her great-grandchildren.

She did not go back to work at the bank.

Oklahoma and Texas are the featured venues for most bank robbery stories, and the two states had more than their share of men who lived simply by taking what other men earned and killing them if they objected. I've left Illinois out of this book; Chicago alone, that sump of crookedness, would fill at least one volume.

But other states suffered from the predators, if not as often or with as much fanfare. Northfield, Minnesota, had its famous visitation from the James-Younger Gang in 1876—the town gets its place elsewhere in this book—and the Northfield men proved themselves tougher than the most famous outlaw gang in American history. They trounced that famous gang, killed two of them, wounded most of the rest, and drove them off in wild flight.

And there were other towns that proved more than even professional bank robbers could handle. Take, for example, Menomonie, Wisconsin, another placid small town with little crime of any consequence—until the morning of October 20, 1931.

That day is special in Menomonie's history, for that was the day when a band of hard-core bank robbers came calling, with designs on the Kraft State Bank. It was quite a gaggle of big names in the outlaw world. There was Tommy Keating (a Chicago boy) and another hood named Tommy Holden. Keating had gotten twenty-five years in the federal pen at Leavenworth for mail robbery.

Keating didn't want to stick around for that long, so he and Holden simply walked out of the prison one day on the strength of a couple of trusty passes. These were stolen, and the story goes that they were provided to Keating and Holden by none other than criminal headliner Machine Gun Kelly.

Keating and Holden picked on the Twin Cities as their base and laid plans to knock over the Kraft Bank. They figured they needed more punks with guns for this one, so they recruited a couple of men with lots of experience.

They were well familiar with the stars of the underworld, for at various time Keating had run with most famous outlaws of the day. One was Jelly Nash, who would be killed in the Kansas City massacre, and the others were the same level of felon, Freddie Barker and Alvin "Creepy" Karpis. Nobody of that bright magnitude was available, so Keating turned to the next best echelon of punk.

This time the getaway car was driven by one Frank Webber, who would stay in the car—a big Lincoln—and keep the engine running. A touch of professionalism there; the criminal mind did not always extend to pre-planning details like that. Webber was apparently a long-time lawbreaker, who was connected, or so the papers said, with a notorious shooter named, somewhat incongruously, Bubbling Over Dever. Bubbling Over was then in the slammer for diamond robbery, so he wasn't available. The fourth man was to be Charles Harmon, also a career thug who had done time down in Texas and in the federal pen at Leavenworth.

At first the robbery appeared to be a resounding success. Although Keating and his boys entered the bank shortly after it opened, there were customers already present. They were being served by Kraft himself, a couple of sons, a daughter, a cousin, and three other employees. The money was available, and the bandits got something in the neighborhood of $130,000. Even though it was mostly in non-negotiable securities, it was a fine payday, but Keating was greedy.

They didn't believe Kraft when he told them they already had all the money there was. So they shot one of his sons by way of encouraging production, and when they got the same explanation from the desperate father, they shot the other son twice. He would survive the big .45 slugs, but nobody could know that at the time. There was no sign of Robin Hood among the invaders of the Kraft Bank, and worse was to come.

There was still another snag, for the bank's alarm went off, and it was loud enough for the getaway driver to hear a half block away. It had been fired by a security officer, who watched the whole thing from an observation post high up in the bank. He said afterward that he did not fire on the bandits because he feared hitting the staff or the customers.

Webber knew there was big trouble when he heard the alarm, so he raced down the street, stopped in front of the bank, and went into action. Now in 1931, anybody with $250 could buy a Thompson submachine gun—by mail, if you wanted to—and the gang had taken one along for its intimidation value. Webber opened both the passenger-side doors and sprayed a few bursts up and down the street to discourage anybody who might choose to interrupt the robbery.

Webber had good reason for his anxiety. People were already converging on the bank, and it was obviously time to go. In a hurry, Keating and his two helpers ran out of the bank, herding one wounded Kraft son and a woman teller ahead of them. She stumbled and fell, and as the others ran toward the car, she seized the opportunity and ran for it. She got away, but the wounded son was forced into the car.

But before they could roar away, the robbers found themselves in the middle of a war. The bank guard, with most of the innocents now out of the line of fire, opened up from the roof. He probably got a round into one of the bandits and certainly put a hole in the gas tank of the getaway car. And the citizenry was now firing on the bewildered outlaws from all directions. A restaurant owner blazed away through his own plate-glass window, another man fired from a second-story window, and still another put a bullet through the rear window.

Webber was trying to return the citizens' fire, but he wasn't hitting anything. And either then or shortly afterward, somebody got a bullet into Webber, a wound to one eye, which would prove fatal. The bandits managed to roar out of town, but only to run head-on into a second firefight a little way down the road.

There an undersheriff fired on the car, and one of the occupants was seen to slump over; the driver—that would be Webber— was "bleeding profusely from the mouth." The Lincoln kept on going at high speed, however, its occupants strewing handfuls of nails in the road to try to hold up pursuit. It didn't work. The townspeople hurriedly formed a posse, climbed into their own cars, and pursued. Down the road, some eight miles from town, they found what was left of Webber; his "right eye and temple were torn by a bullet," as a local paper reported, and he was very dead. His steel vest and two revolvers hadn't done him a bit of good. Beside him was another steel vest, some indication that still another bandit had been wounded. The paper went into great detail about the corpse, right down to the tattoo of a naked lady on one arm and the double eagle sewed on his underwear (that was supposed to mean some connection to either Germany or Austria).

Tragically, the pursuers also discovered the body of the hostage, shot in the back of the head. That just lent further impetus to the pursuit over six counties. And in time the pursuers discovered the body of Harmon, shot in the neck and knee. One tale of the robber says his comrades abandoned Harmon while he was still alive, leaving him a "supply of bandages and iodine" and some securities just in case he stayed alive . . . you wonder whether they were negotiable.

Along with Harmon's body the pursuers found the tommy gun and a couple of pistols. But they could not come up with the survivors. The outlaws had taken the precaution of stashing cans of gasoline here and there to quickly refill the tank without going into nosy service stations. And finally the getaway car turned up, burned up, without any sign of the outlaws. Enough remained that the pursuers could determine that the back seat was blood-soaked and the rear window shot out.

The search for the robbers extended all over the country. Somebody even interviewed Creepy Karpis—he was easy to find, his address being Alcatraz—but if Karpis knew anything, he wasn't telling the law. Back at Menomonie the two dead outlaws were on display at the funeral parlor, but nobody claimed them or even showed an interest besides the curious public.

But the two surviving bandits did not have long to enjoy their loot. In less than a year, the FBI got them both, ignominiously enough on a golf course in Kansas City. The story goes that career robber Jelly Nash was playing with them but was such a lousy golfer that he was deep in the rough when his playing partners were pinched. He at least had about a year of freedom left. Keating and Holden did not. They had already started serving life sentences . . . and died in prison.

Similar things happened all across the country, from Meeker, Colorado, to Southwest City, Texas, to Bodie, California. Again and again it was finally the citizens who rose up and hammered the outlaws. The local folk had built this great nation, and they were going to hold it.

Chapter 13

SUAVE ROBBERS

The Con Men

AT FIRST GLANCE THESE white-collar crooks don't appear to belong here with the robbers, with violent men, shooters and such, since the average scam artists avoided violence like the plague. It was very bad for business, and besides, it was dangerous. The con man got his dollars peacefully, by deceit, without killing folks to get a payday—except, of course, for the occasional suicide and the pitiful victims of the medical cons. And he didn't have to take mortal risks himself, which was doubly important to the swindler.

Selling somebody a gold brick has long been a sort of synonym for swindling, but it really happened, and happened repeatedly. As late as 1939, in fact, a couple of sophisticated Texas bankers fell for this scam, parting with a cool three hundred thousand dollars . . . for a brick. This scam had been going on for a very long time, and the stock-in-trade was little more than a cast-metal or even an ordinary brick, prettily gilded, of course.

The finishing touch, in case the buyer wanted an assay, was a plug of real gold in the phony brick; you could pry out all or part of the plug from the brick and give that to the assayer. And presto!—it assayed correctly. The really professional con man used his own—phony—assayer whenever possible, but he could also come up with real gold to assay at need.

The con fraternity was almost a family and boasted some of the most amazing nicknames in the West, which is saying quite a lot, considering the violent outlaws' contrived handles. There was the Christ Kid, virtuous on Sunday but crooked as hell the rest of the week. Others included the High-Ass Kid, Farmer Brown, Slobbering Bob, Cockroach Gary, Brickyard Jimmy, Pretty Billy, Soapy Smith, and Big and Little Alabama. And there were a host of others with equally engaging names.

Usually they worked together, but there was the occasional falling-out, over turf or a woman. On at least one occasion, it was simply an angry argument about something or other. In the end one man was so obnoxious to the other that the second con man pulled a pistol and blew him away, proving conclusively that it can be terminally stupid to bring a mouth to a gunfight.

Mining was the happy hunting ground for swindlers, not just the small-time claims salters but owners of large mines. They would stage a large discovery in their mines and announce it in triumph, thereby driving up the price of their shares. They then sold high, and when the bonanza pooped out, they could buy again . . . low, of course.

There were somewhat cruder attempts to inflate the value of a silver claim. One group of snakes used the crude method of pouring bits of melted silver dollars down their worthless shaft—it worked, too, until somebody looked closely enough to distinguish the occasional Indian head among the rest of the "high-grade ore." By then, of course, it was too late.

In at least one case, what went around really did come around, when a crook called Chicken Bill salted a hole in the ground with silver and then managed to sell the property to Colorado mining magnate Horace Tabor. When Tabor found nothing in the shaft, Chicken Bill told Tabor about the hoax—at least till Tabor drove the worthless shaft down further and hit silver.

There were far more elaborate scams. The simplest of these involved selling something the con man didn't own, like the

Statue of Liberty or the Brooklyn Bridge, which was sold over and over again. An industrious Turk sold the Galata Bridge across the Golden Horn off Constantinople, and both the Tower of London and Buckingham Palace changed hands.

Probably the most elaborate, longest-lived scam of all time was the quest for Sir Francis Drake's fortune. The father of this one was an American, who kept it going for years on the money contributed by people he'd sold on the idea that they were heirs to Drake's gold, millions and million of dollars of it. He spent much time in England, sending wonderful messages back to his contributors about all the encouraging developments in the case and all the obstacles he had to overcome.

That charade went on until a British policeman produced Drake's will, probated centuries before. Whatever inheritance there had been was long ago distributed. The news put a serious crimp in the swindler's plans, and it got worse when he returned to the States. He went to prison.

Then there were the usual "white-collar" scams, which relied again on the credulous nature of frontier Americans. These folks both wanted to get rich quick and were inclined to trust folks, to take other Americans at face value and believe what they said. And gamble with them.

The shell game was as old as time and took no special equipment: just a pea and three walnut shells—step right up, gentlemen, just follow the pea as I shuffle the shells; watch the little pea and when you guess which shell it ended under, you win. And so on. Only the pea wasn't under any of the shells, having been switched out by the swindler, often simply scooped up under his fingernails, carefully kept long for the purpose.

The old shell game became slightly more civilized with the substitution of a tiny ball and three thimbles for the walnut shells and the pea—the operators were called "thimbleriggers" after that, but the scam remained the same. That was also true of the venerable game of three-card monte. Monte followed the same principle: "The hand is quicker than the eye, gentlemen—or is it?"

In this case the operator shuffled three cards around on a flat surface, face down. The winning card, normally a red queen, won for you if you could follow its travels through the deft movements and endless patter of the con man. And there was a variation on this swindle: a shill standing by who won a couple of times—they let the mark win at least once, too. And then the shill whispered to the sucker that he saw a tiny crease in the queen. And maybe there was, but it was gone and another card creased by the time he got his big bet down.

And then there was rigged poker, played with a cold deck provided by the con man, of course. There was a thriving business in manufacturing cards for the purpose, one of the makers being a college professor, who sold his useful creations for the bargain price of thirty-six dollars a dozen. Loaded dice were everywhere, and roulette wheels rigged with a brake the con man could work with his stomach or, later on, by electricity.

Banco traveled to America from Britain and is probably the ancestor of the word "bunco." It was simply a set of numbered spaces painted on a cloth surface; the number of spaces varied depending on whether you were using cards or dice, and you simply bet on which numbers would show up. In either case the sucker lost, because the cards were marked and the dice loaded.

There was even a novel game called thirty-one, played with or without dice. The sucker and the dealer called a number up to six alternately, and it did not matter much who made the first call. What the dealer knew, and the sucker did not, was that if a player counted so that the number he called, added to the total already called, reached three, ten, seventeen, or twenty-four, he could not beaten.

Magic machines drew some supposedly more sophisticated suckers, like the Gold Accumulator, which would attract overnight the particles of gold supposed to be suspended in saltwater. Of course it worked, since the operator of that one was an accomplished swimmer, who paddled out at night to swap a gold-crusted duplicate for the original accumulator. The cagey con artist who thought that one up simply sold shares in his process . . . and ultimately disappeared.

And then there was an absolutely foolproof con that protected the sucker from those hateful radio waves, which could cause who knew what horrible maladies. The sucker paid to face a mysterious machine—the Radio Opposer—that gave him or her protection against whatever malevolent emanations came out of the ether.

That wasn't the end of the con. The mark then bought a supply of magic pills that continued the protection. They were made of bicarbonate of soda, and if they didn't accomplish anything, they didn't hurt either. The wonderful part of this con was that it worked; sure enough, the sucker was never attacked by radio waves. The con man's fee was obviously money well spent.

The medical cons produced some of the foulest of the con artists. Doc Fowler could diagnose a patient's ills simply by holding the sufferer's hand; Fowler boasted that he'd cured some four thousand cancer patients. God alone knows how many people died who might have been saved by going to a real doctor. The same was true of a charlatan who could diagnose you when you weren't even around, concentrating his mighty intellect on you long-distance at a time prearranged.

They were in the same category as the soulless peddler of "tuberclide." In a time when tuberculosis was a widespread scourge, thousands of desperate people—many of them parents of very sick kids—laid out thousands of hard-earned dollars on this wholly worthless nostrum.

Magic medical machines abounded. There were the Davis Kidder Magneto, the Dynomizer, the Radioclast, the Natural Eye Normalizer, and the Magno-Electric Vitalizer, for example, and that was only scratching the surface. They generally revolved around the mystery of electricity, which the average person understood only generally or not at all—like radio waves.

Best of all were the wonderful diagnoses performed with the Radioclast, which depended on dialing in various specific frequencies known only to the inventor and those doctors to whom he

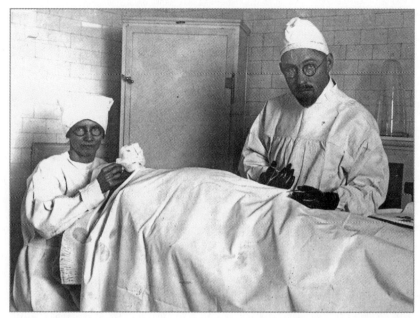

Dr. Goat Gland Brinkley.

KANSAS STATE HISTORICAL SOCIETY

revealed them—for a price. The machine did the rest. Hydrotherapy was a simpler treatment, devised, it was said, by an Austrian farmer who had healed his own fractured ribs with cold water compresses.

There was a whole world of patent medicines if you wanted to dose yourself, like the Infallible Worm-Destroying Lozenges or the Vegetable Nervous Cordial. And if that didn't work—and it surely wouldn't—you could try some stuff marketed by the Kickapoo Indian Medicine Company and dose yourself with the original Snake Oil, perhaps significantly made in New York City.

Or maybe the Chill and Ague Eliminator would cure what ailed you. And if that didn't work, you could move on to a phrenologist or engage a practitioner of bloodletting. And on and on. At least most of the so-called medicines and magic treatments wouldn't kill you.

Right off, anyhow.

The most engaging of the medical quacks was Dr. John Romulus Brinkley, less formally known as Goat Gland Brinkley. If you were a man dissatisfied with your performance, you could have Dr. Brinkley insert the organs of a billy goat at the appropriate spot, thus rejuvenating your system. Apparently there were lots of folks disappointed—or disappointing—in the bedroom, and they flocked to Brinkley's door, all intent on recovering what they once had, or thought they had.

Never mind that some of them never had been much in that line of effort, but they thought they were, and that was enough to bring them to Brinkley's door. Or perhaps they just wanted to improve their performance. Any of these notions produced a clamor for goat glands, and was ready-made for Brinkley's extensive practice.

He was a busy man and amassed a fortune from quackery. At one point he boasted that he was running out of goats, and in fact it appears that he performed literally thousands of his "restorative" surgeries. He also had a subspecialty somewhat mysteriously called "prostate softening," about which the less said the better.

They don't make 'em like Doc Brinkley any more, which is probably just as well. At least he wasn't working on sick kids.

Chapter 14

PRO

Harvey Bailey

IN SHARP CONTRAST TO Wilber Underhill, the psychopathic fumbler who appears in the chapter called "Thug," Harvey Bailey was the real professional robber. He was probably the most thorough planner ever to case and rob a bank and then disappear to actually enjoy his considerable stash of booty uncaught. Harvey John Bailey was a contemporary of Underhill, maybe the only man on earth Underhill respected, but the contrast between the two men could not have been more dramatic.

Where Underhill was a brutal bully who disliked almost everybody and especially hated police officers, Bailey got along with almost everybody and was particularly careful that no one got hurt in any of his robberies if he could help it. How much of this was the milk of human kindness and how much was fear of the electric chair is open to question, but Bailey was far from the vicious killer that was Wilber Underhill.

Boastful, arrogant Henry Starr was called the King of the Bank Robbers, and he, at least, was convinced that he was exactly that. "I've robbed more banks than any other man," he said, or something like that, and the papers inflated Starr's image still further.

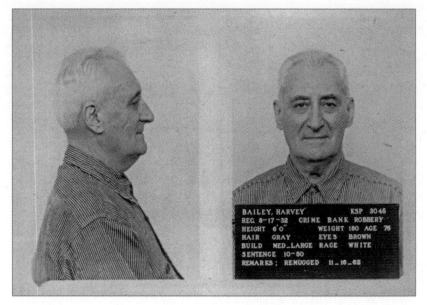

BAILEY, HARVEY   KSP 3045
REG. 8-17-32   CRIME BANK ROBBERY
HEIGHT 6'0"   WEIGHT 180 AGE 76
HAIR   GRAY   EYES   BROWN
BUILD   MED.-LARGE   RACE   WHITE
SENTENCE 10-50
REMARKS ;   REMUGGED   11-16-62

Robbery as an art: Harvey Bailey.

KANSAS STATE HISTORICAL SOCIETY

And Starr did indeed rob a lot of banks, but he also spent a good deal of time in various prisons, got himself shot twice, and eventually was killed following the robbery business.

Bailey, on the other hand, took great care that nobody got shot on his jobs; he was, for example, very careful of Underhill, although they cooperated from time to time. He knew what Underhill was and wanted no part of the killing Underhill liked so well. And no man in the robbery trade took more care in preparing for a bank job than Bailey did. He is said to have had an uncanny sort of photographic memory, which he used to casually view the interior layout of a bank and remember every important detail after just one visit.

He carried over his careful planning to the raid itself, and beyond, to the all-important getaway, writing out each turn of the road and the precise distance to the next change of direction. And he preferred using what he called the "cat roads," the less traveled back roads of the countryside. They were unpaved as a rule, thick with dust in dry weather and bogs when the rains came. But they had a couple of great values to a bank robber on the run.

First, you could go anywhere on them, and you had your choice of routes. Second, miserable though the going was, the few paved roads were easy enough for the police to watch and block. They could not nearly be everywhere on the cat roads, and they had no way of knowing which of them the escaping robbers might choose. And when Bailey had finished his painstaking reconnaissance, he generally knew more about the back roads than the pursuers.

His careful advance planning got him through twenty-nine confirmed robberies, maybe more. Bailey might well have run free for the rest of his life and escaped the misery of twelve years in Alcatraz. For, as will appear, it was a fluke that got him there, a terminally stupid mistake by somebody else that got him sent to the Rock.

With a batch of other professional hoodlums, Bailey had robbed the bank in Fort Scott, Kansas; part of the loot was in negotiable bonds, and that's what ultimately got Bailey in trouble. The other men, frequent practitioners of the gentle art of robbery, were hard and experienced. They included multiple murderer Larry DeVol, Alvin "Creepy" Karpis, one of Ma Barker's egregious sons, Freddie, and veteran outlaws Tommie Holden and Red Phillips.

The trouble began innocently enough, just before, of all things, a game of golf. Part of the gang waited to begin their round of golf until the conclusion of a meeting to arrange the sale of the bonds to a fence. When the deal with the fence was made, not only was the price lower than the bandits expected and wanted, but for some reason one five-hundred-dollar bond—part of DeVol's share—could not be moved.

Bailey and several of the others had a game scheduled at the Old Mission golf course in Kansas City, and as they hurried to tee off, Bailey took the troublesome bond and shoved it in his pocket. He can't have given the action his usual careful thought; had he done so, he might well have at least guessed at the vast amount of trouble that would come to him from that single piece of embossed paper.

Bailey usually ran with the best and most active robbers in the business, and so he had with this group of long-time pros. Larry DeVol was one of the veterans, among other things murderer of a police officer in Kirksville, Missouri, and long-time safecracker. DeVol was the worst of a bad lot, who finished his earthly race on the dirty end of a policeman's bullet. Before the world was rid of him—at only thirty-two—he was responsible for the deaths of eleven people, six of them lawmen.

As early as 1929, DeVol met the noxious Alvin Karpis—in prison, from which the two escaped. Recaptured in 1930, he was back doing what he did best, and in March of 1932 reached the big time of crime when he joined other charter members of what came to be called the Barker-Karpis Gang in their first major crime. It was a whopping score for the time, more than a quarter million dollars in cash and bonds. In October of the same year, he was in on a Minnesota bank robbery that netted a paltry forty-four hundred dollars. To these high livers, that was just walkin'-around money.

And finally, just four days before Christmas, he was captured in St. Paul and ultimately convicted of both robbery and murder. The sentence was life, but he was later moved to an asylum. He escaped and went back to his usual profession of robbery, until the summer of 1936, when he fought the law in Enid, Oklahoma, and this time the law won. Sadly, a police officer died, too, before this thoroughly worthless hoodlum went down.

Among other Bailey confederates was Francis Keating, called Jimmy. He was part of the gang arrested with Bailey on the Kansas City golf course, along with his long-time buddy Tom Holden, with whom he had escaped from prison in early 1928, using passes forged and provided by one George Kelly, later known as Machine Gun Kelly. Kelly, by the way, as a big-time hoodlum was largely the creation of the press. Until, that is, his involvement with others in the kidnapping of an Oklahoma oilman, which brought in a ransom of a cool two hundred thousand dollars. He is credited with creating a new word in law enforcement, allegedly pleading with arresting U.S. officers, "Don't shoot, G-men." In fact, the term had been around for a while before Kelly said it, if he did (or maybe it was his wife, Kathryn), but it made a good story.

Raymond Hamilton was another big name in the sport of robbery. He was another Oklahoma boy, who ran with Clyde Barrow for a while and at last fell into the hands of the law and was sentenced—for robbery and murder—to a mere 263 years in the Texas prison system. He escaped early in 1934 with several other hoodlums, using pistols allegedly furnished by Clyde Barrow and killing a prison guard in the process. Recaptured within three months, he was sentenced to death for his latest murder.

Once more he escaped using smuggled pistols—you have to wonder about prison security—but he remained free for less than a year. This time there was no escaping, only execution. The Texas authorities did not dally: Hamilton was dead a month later. Like so many other outlaws, he suffered from a cranial vacuum: Both escapes were from confinement in Texas, but Hamilton did not have the brains to leave that state. It cost him his life.

The Cookson Hills have been mentioned more than once in this narrative, and some of the cast of depraved men who robbed and killed with the Cooksons as their base of operations. One writer—a master of research—estimates that criminals from the Cookson Hills were involved in at least thirty-six robberies between late 1931 and the end of 1934, which of course doesn't count what other lawbreakers were doing who weren't Cookson based.

So the Cookson boys were busy indeed, but there were more, many more, besides the big names; and if they weren't anybody you'd invite to dinner anytime soon, they make interesting reading.

Early in 1934 the apparently omnipresent robber Ford Bradshaw hit another bank, this one up in Wellington, Kansas, and as usual he had a good deal of help. Two of them were the Eno boys, Clarence and Otis, criminals with much experience. They hid out in Tulsa and were incautious enough that Bradshaw was seen entering the building. The Tulsa police raided the house, armed to the teeth with automatic weapons, phosphorus grenades, and tear gas.

The Eno boys were apprehended and carted off to jail, but the officers missed Bradshaw, who had the luck to be someplace else. Three women also went into the bag: Otis' wife, another woman, and the Eno boys' aged mother, Mary, matriarch of a family that rivaled the Underhills for the Jukes-Kallikak award.

Otis and Clarence seemed likely to go the way of three other sons, who were also in prison at the same time. Sure enough, Otis and Clarence left the courthouse on their way to do twenty to one hundred in the pen. Their foul record had caught up with them with a bang. They did not get out of prison until the mid-'50s.

That same month police down in Sapulpa, Oklahoma, got an anonymous tip that several "suspicious" men were holed up in a two-room shack just outside the town. Since the area had been haunted by several recent gas station robberies, the sheriff staged a raid that rivaled in blood anything else in recent memory even in that violent era. Two lawmen died, and so did one Delbert Carolan, a jewel thief, and a veteran hoodlum called Aussie Elliot, a long-time follower of Pretty Boy Floyd. Badly wounded was still another robber, Eldon Wilson, who had a dozen or more holes in him.

Anger ran so high against Wilson that the governor, Alfalfa Bill Murray, sent in the National Guard to help the outnumbered police protect Wilson from the ire of a mob that numbered in the hundreds. It was all for naught, for Wilson was dead of his wounds before noon the next day. Now Bradshaw and his cohort Charlie Cotner were at the top of the list, right up there with Pretty Boy Floyd. The frustrated forces of law and order didn't have long to wait.

The lawmen mounted a major operation, beating the bushes in the Cookson Hills, but they missed Bradshaw and Cotner, as well as their other chief target, Floyd. Nevertheless, the drive netted a number of other wanted men without any major casualties to the law. The hunt went on.

Then on March 3, 1934, officers from Fort Smith and LaFlore County responded to a call about trouble in a joint near Arkoma. When they got there, they were met by the owner, who told them that a man had been holding captive a whole bar full of people, robbing them and waving a .45 pistol around, apparently upset because he'd lost some money gambling in the same roadhouse. His revenge routine included destroying the bar's slot machines with a baseball bat.

He was engaged in taking his anger out on still another harmless slot machine when the officers appeared. They made the arrest and included a woman who was along with their quarry. They handcuffed him, took custody of his gun, and got a bonus in the form of his steel vest, not the sort of waistcoat you find every day. Obviously, the officers had stumbled on a bad man.

They had. The vandal was Ford Bradshaw, full of coffin varnish and resentment. At first he seemed to be willing to come along with them quietly, but as the arresting officers started to take him to a police car, Bradshaw suddenly struck LaFlore County deputy Bob Harper in the face and ran. He dashed on toward the door, knocking officers out of the way as he ran, but Harper wasn't having any of that.

The deputy drew his .45 and put three bullets in Bradshaw's back. And then, to make sure, he walked up to the fallen outlaw, stood over him, and pointed the .45 at his chest. "Don't do that," said Bradshaw, but Harper did that. He did that twice more, and that was the end of the road for the fearsome Bradshaw.

There was some public unhappiness about the circumstances surrounding the departure of a handcuffed outlaw, especially about the last two rounds, but Harper said he thought Bradshaw was running to get a shotgun from his car. Sure enough, there was indeed a sawed-off shotgun in the car, along with a good deal of ammo, two pistols, and a rifle. Still, that didn't quiet the criticism; the thing got far enough that Harper was charged with homicide.

But Bradshaw was generally detested in the law enforcement community. "He was mean and would shoot you," said one officer simply, and Bradshaw's record confirmed the cop's judgment: When Harper rid the world of him, Bradshaw was suspected in at least ten robberies and half that many murders.

A local preacher gave a namby-pamby sermon at the well-attended funeral, a good deal of stuff about poor old Bradshaw not having a chance. The judge felt otherwise, dismissing the charges with a few choice comments about how no court would find Harper guilty for killing a lowlife like Bradshaw.

The action went on, this time around Sapulpa, where police made a rich haul when they raided a farm near Mannford. This was, as the miners used to say, real pay dirt, because among those collected—fortunately, without a fight—was the elusive Charlie Cotner, along with several other wanted men, at least one of whom was a part of the murderous gang headed by Doc Barker.

Once the court was finished with him, Cotner would cease to be a menace to honest folks' money.

The incriminating evidence the officers found was a bonus, and it was more than ample: nitroglycerine, said to amount to something like two quarts; morphine and syringes; and counterfeit money. Most interesting of all were a dozen safes, open of course, from various banks.

That was May 1934, and then in June hoodlum Jim Benge was tried for the murder of Susie Sharpe during an abortive carjacking of a family automobile. He went away for life, and the judge said he wished it could have been the electric chair. Too bad it wasn't, and the only reason it wasn't was that the jury couldn't bring themselves to recommend it.

Later that same year Ed Davis, one of Wilber Underhill's running mates, fled to sunny California to try crime there. He did, and it didn't work very well. Introduced to the California prison system, he didn't like it much. He joined in an escape, which succeeded only in producing a bloodbath in which a prison warden and a guard were murdered. That got him a one-way trip to death row, and the world was a little cleaner still.

October saw the event of the year in law enforcement. The idol of the criminal world, the closest approach to Robin Hood the era offered, took on Melvin Purvis and the FBI and came in second. Charles Arthur Floyd—Pretty Boy—died ingloriously in a farmer's field up in Ohio. The world of newspaper reporters was devastated, dozens of simpering women lost their heartthrob, and a whole legion of wannabe hoodlums were deprived of their role model.

Floyd's last act was his best one, for Pretty Boy came back home to the Cookson Hills to be the centerpiece of a huge funeral. An estimated thirty thousand people attended the happening, and afterward his memory lingered on in the hearts of people who thought he was indeed Robin Hood reincarnated, or just didn't like laws and bankers. But his passing marked the end of an era, or at least the beginning of its end.

Dillinger bit the dust in Chicago in 1934, and Bonnie and Clyde "went out together"—as they swore they'd do—in the same year, the honors done by a group of lawmen led by Frank Hamer. Bonnie got her wish, as she had prophesied in her poetry—"death for Bonnie and Clyde," she wrote, and so it was.

The officers ambushed the pair and opened fire without any of this modern-day frippery of "Throw up your hands; you're under arrest." Knowing Clyde Barrow was given to killing people who got in the way, the law simply blazed away, firing maybe 150 rounds into the outlaws' car.

When the smoke blew away and the officers inspected the car, they found the interior splashed with blood and dotted with bits of the occupants. The armament they found at the same time sure validated Hamer's decision to open fire without the futile rigama-role of an invitation to surrender. The two outlaws had loaded their car with three automatic rifles, ten or twelve pistols, a couple of sawed-off shotguns, an enormous store of ammunition, and fifteen pairs of stolen license plates. Perhaps significantly, the officers also found a copy of Walter Noble Burns' *Saga of Billy the Kid*.

In 1935 it was the turn of the vile Barker family. Ma Barker and her son Freddie, as the song says, "fought the law and the law won," and inept Doc got himself killed trying to escape from Alcatraz.

The world was a whole lot cleaner place.

Chapter 15

THUG

Wilber Underbill and the Cookson Hills Boys

THE COOKSON HILLS OF EASTERN Oklahoma have been mentioned more than once in this history, for they were refuge and R & R site for a couple of generations of the most lethal hoodlums in the history of American crime.

There wasn't a whole lot of money out in the hills. Hardscrabble farming and moonshining were the major forms of employment. And because hooch cooking was illegal, the "laws," as people called the police and revenue agents, were downright unpopular. The number of young men who committed crimes for a living was multiplied several times by the number of friends and kin that also lived in the hills. That meant that the robbers never lacked for hiding places, food, and willing lookouts.

The depravity of the many outlaw denizens of the Cooksons is fairly illustrated by the Sharp family tragedy. Mrs. Sharp was a passenger in a car with her daughter and her daughter's small daughter, two young cousins, and her son Owen, who was driving. They were on their way home not far from Muskogee when Owen saw somebody shining a flashlight at him from the roadside ahead. The next thing he saw were several men with guns by the side of the road, and he knew he was looking at a carjacking . . . or worse.

Young Owen hit the gas and roared past this menacing lot, but as he did so, the night flamed with gunfire. At least a dozen bullets tore into the car and into his mother, his sister, her daughter, and a young cousin. His sister was in obvious pain, and his mother was crumpled and motionless.

Owen kept the hammer down and got clear of the ambush, then drove on until he won through to a service station. There the police and an ambulance were called, but it was too late for Mrs. Sharp. She was dead on arrival at the hospital, and her daughter, hit three times, teetered on the brink of death before she finally pulled through. By the grace of God, the two kids were not badly injured.

In spite of the violence common to the Cooksons, the callous ambush of the family aroused much anger, and the temper of the people was not helped by more hijackings, fortunately without any more murders. Lawmen flooded the area with posses that may have totaled as many as a hundred men.

They came up dry, but the "laws" stayed with it. One of the major suspects was Kie Carlile, twice convicted of armed robbery, along with a prison buddy, Troy Love, who, in spite of looking goofy in the extreme, was also a two-time loser.

The two began to run with four other men as worthless as they, including professional criminal Ford Bradshaw—a prison buddy of the ultimate thug, Wilber Underhill. He was joined by three others just as bad: Jim Benge, Van Ratliff, and Ed Clanton. Bradshaw and company went to robbing and, it now appeared, getting drunk, carjacking, and killing innocent motorists.

Their days were numbered, for among other lawmen pursuing these hoodlums was Cherokee County deputy Grover Bishop, a very bad man to have hunting you. The story goes that he found one Carter, Carlile's cousin, loaded down with groceries and other supplies, and began to question him, convinced the food was intended for Carlile. When he got no cooperation, Grover simply threatened to hang Carter, or maybe he actually did . . . temporarily.

Wilber Underhill on one of his better days.

KANSAS STATE HISTORICAL SOCIETY

Anyhow, he got his information, and Carlile and Troy Love soon became extinct.

Jim Benge ended up beaten to death by the side of a road, Clanton died of a police bullet, and Ratliff went off to prison. Mrs. Sharp was avenged, as far as the law could do it, but other unfinished jobs awaited. One was the vile Wilber Underhill.

At the height of the bank robbers' heyday—the '20s and '30s—no single man of that fraternity was better publicized, or more cordially detested, than Underhill. His sensational newspaper title was the Tri-State Terror, and for once an outlaw deserved the damning title.

He came out of agricultural country in southwest Missouri, one of seven children of a perpetually struggling family. Tiring of hard work in the fields, his father moved into town, just the place not to raise a punk kid like Wilber, especially since the move did not appreciably advance the family's financial status.

However unsuccessful the family was, they were certainly prolific. There were seven kids, four of them brothers, and the old man didn't set them much of an example. Continuing largely penniless, arrested for petty theft and disturbing the peace, Wilber's father passed to his reward at forty-six.

That left mama Almira to take care of the family, and the task was far beyond her. Except, of course, for acquiring the habit of forever proclaiming that her sons were spotless little innocents and that whatever they were accused of was a frame-up. She was good at that; she should have been, for Wilber gave her lots of opportunity for practice.

By his early teens Wilber's brother Ernest was running wild. One night, when he and some other delinquents finished robbing one man of a pitiful $2.96, they brought on a major clash with the law with the attempted holdup of an old man who sold peanuts and tamales for a living. When he objected to having his meager resources torn away from him, Ernest shot and killed him.

Enough people talked about the crime that Ernest was run down and sent to prison for life. There he would make his home, save for a few short months, for the rest of his days. Since he was constantly in trouble in the prison, he effectively denied himself any chance at parole.

Wilber may have been with the other punks the night Ernest wantonly killed the old tamale vendor, but he was thought to have been no more than along for the ride. He was not prosecuted; that was yet to come.

Wilber had managed to be under a falling case of bottles while he was still in his teens. The result was a fractured skull, and the story goes that he was never the same afterward. It is not clear what he was not the same as, or what that meant to the people who knew him.

Maybe his busted crown was the root of all his later trouble; the chances are better that it was just his vile nature, for Wilber managed to demonstrate in his later life that he was probably at least a sociopath, if not out-and-out psychotic.

The lump on his head didn't stop Wilber (or Wilbur, as he spelled his given name) from embarking on a new career, burglary. His brother Ernest, meanwhile, was a bootlegger up Kansas City way, and brother George was already getting into trouble at sixteen, also as an amateur burglar in the family's hometown of Joplin. George got lucky with a suspended sentence because of his youth.

Then in 1920 couples started getting robbed at gunpoint in a lover's lane near Joplin. The police arranged a dummy necking party featuring a detective and a female volunteer, while two other cops hid in the bushes. It was crude, but it worked, for the bandit showed up, waving a gun and demanding money. Only, when summoned to surrender, the intruder opened fire, and in the ensuing gunfight escaped, apparently wounded. And sure enough, when officers raided a shack on a tip several days later, who should they find but Wilber, complete with flesh wound.

Wilber's trial was a fairly commonplace affair, except for his mother's repeated protestations that her son was the victim of a police plot. It was also noteworthy for a spectator's midtrial identification—in the courtroom—of brother George as a man who had robbed him. George confirmed his guilt by taking it on the heel and toe, as the saying went, and disappearing abruptly from the courtroom.

Wilber spent some time up the river doing graduate work in crime, and on his release lost no time in getting back to his career, in this case a gas station robbery. As always, he loudly proclaimed his innocence, with his mother and sister as a sort of Greek chorus supporting him. That didn't impress the court, perhaps in part because when searched prior to his preliminary hearing, Wilber was found to have one hacksaw blade sewed into his shorts and another one in one shoe.

Back to jail he went, where he had regular visits from mama and brother George, who brought him good things to eat and tobacco to smoke. They also resupplied him with hacksaw blades to cut some more. His work on his bars was discovered before he was finished, however, and Wilber was transferred to a high-security cell. Not me, said Wilber, it must have been somebody who occupied the cell before I did. Perhaps significantly, his mother had only recently brought him a bucket of molasses.

He got five years and joined brother Ernest in prison. It was quite a family reunion, especially when George joined them—doing two years for larceny. And the circle was complete when brother Earl started serving his five years for burglary. Now mother Almira could visit everybody in the same day.

Wilber got out in the fall of 1926, after one rather messy try at escape by crawling through a sewer. He traveled to Picher, Oklahoma, then a hub of mining activity, and got a job. Labor in the mines was, however, too much like work, and so he went back to what he did best, palling up with a punk named Ike Akins, called Skeet.

The two went a-robbing, and in the process Wilber shot a sixteen-year-old boy, whose only offense was trying to run. With a bullet in one lung, the lad barely made it, and the two thugs went on to stick up a couple of small businesses. They also tried to roll a miner, and when he resisted, they shot him in the face. Luckily, the wound was only a graze.

Akins and Wilber then moved their operations to Okmulgee, where they staged a drugstore robbery and killed another man. His sin was ignoring their command to raise his hands, thinking what he was seeing was some sort of joke. The police arrested the pair shortly thereafter, and a couple of eyewitnesses identified them. As usual, Wilber didn't help himself, since he was carrying not one but two revolvers and, not surprisingly, had a couple of his usual hacksaw blades sewed into his clothing.

The two went to jail, but they weren't there long. It seems the ever-fond Almira visited, and not long thereafter Wilber and Akins sawed their way out. Akins was soon caught, and when he was being transported, he tried to escape. The two officers with him weren't having any, and one shot him at least twice in the head.

For the policeman who downed him, it was the third fatal shooting in a single year. Perhaps Akins' end was not entirely consistent with strict notions of due process of law, but it sure saved the state a lot of time and money in holding trials, not to mention associated inconveniences like hung juries, mistrials, and reversals on appeal.

But Wilber stayed on the loose, and back in Picher he showed off his short-fuse temper again during an attempt to arrest him for the robbery of—of all things—a movie theater. A young man trying to help a town constable with the arrest was shot down and killed, but Underhill got away.

His next stops for cash withdrawals were a couple of stores and another service station. It was about this time that Wilber began to be called the Tri-State Terror, and the name stuck. Inevitably somebody else called him a mad dog, and the theater owner, who had held off shooting Underhill because he didn't want to kill over a "few dollars," was now repenting of his mercy and commented that he wished he'd "shot the son of a bitch" when he had the chance.

Wilber now began to make the same stupid mistakes common to men in the outlaw profession. With a girlfriend he started spending, throwing enough cash around that a merchant in the little town of Heavener, Oklahoma, smelled a rat and called the local law. There was apparently also word from an informant somewhere that Wilber was bound for Muskogee by way of the town of Panama, where he and the woman planned to stay the night.

The arrest went smoothly, at least as smoothly as things ever went with Wilber. Encountered on the hotel stairs and summoned to surrender, Wilber reached for a back pocket instead, and one of the officers promptly shot him, putting a bullet through his thigh and taking all the fight out of him. He was convicted in spite of some "poor me" talk by Wilber and the usual harangue by mama, who showed up to rant about her son's innocence and her own penury. Neither her speech nor Wilber's whining helped at all. Wilber got life.

The next stop was the state prison at McAlester, where Wilber took up residence in the summer of 1927. The population at the time read like a "Who's Who" of criminals, what with the likes of

George Kimes, Ed Lockhart, and Clarence Eno all inside at the same time. Even so, Wilber was described by an assistant warden as "the meanest man we have ever had at this institution." He wouldn't work and spent his time cursing at the guards.

And plotting. In 1931 he escaped again, getting clear away although a massive search was launched for him. This time he ended up near Independence, Kansas. While he was there, he married—again. He did that a lot, omitting the customary step of divorce in between adventures into further marital bliss.

All this even though Wilber was quite busy, holding up a drugstore and another movie theater, this one in Coffeyville, Kansas. The story goes that it took a little time for anybody to notice the screams of the theater cashier, the main attraction of the evening being the evil Dracula, in the form of Bela Lugosi.

Wilber also robbed a couple of gas stations, and during the second robbery he killed yet another man. The station owner had whaled the tar out of two previous men who tried to hold him up, but this time he was out of luck. Whatever happened, he was dead by the time medical help got there.

Wilber's next job that we know of was another service station in Wichita, and then for an encore he murdered a Wichita police officer who knocked on his hotel door to check out a report of a couple of "suspicious-looking fellows." The second suspicious-looking fellow was Wilber's young nephew Frank Vance, whom Wilber had brought along to do the driving—something Wilber didn't like to do.

Both men were captured while resting under a tree, apparently tired out from their attempts to escape, and it was off to court for them both. And so, in September 1931, Wilber once more became a number, this time at the Kansas State Prison up at Lansing. Wilber and some other hard cases—several of them alumni of Oklahoma's Big Mac, tough McAlester prison—set about planning an escape.

Their first try was a fizzle, and Wilber ended up spending a good deal of time in solitary. But once out, it was back to plotting. This time somebody ran in several automatic pistols apparently hidden in a bale of hemp, which was used in the prison rope factory. This one worked. Using the warden as a hostage, and armed with their pistols and a couple of homemade shivs, they got clear of the prison during a baseball game.

Most of the escapees went right on with their criminal careers, hitting banks and small businesses. At least two of them were shot down by an alert bank employee when they tried to rob a bank in Altamont, Kansas. One of them died; the other went back to prison. As for Wilber, he and other escapees robbed a bank in Geary, Oklahoma. Two of them were quickly captured, and a third intelligently lit a shuck for California.

Wilber went off to visit a one-time cellmate, who lived in a wide spot in the road deep in the notorious Cookson Hills. If he could feel safe anywhere, it was here, surrounded by people who either were outlaws themselves or had relatives who were, or just plain didn't like laws, or "laws," the guys who enforced them.

Just a year before, the Cooksons had been the scene of two horrific firefights between lawmen and robbers; the death toll totaled seven. This was bootlegging county, which added to the general wariness of the population. Suffice it to say that Wilber fit right in with criminal scum like Mount Cookson, Ford Bradshaw and Cowboy Charlie Cotner, Kie Carlile and vicious Troy Love.

The Cooksons were Wilber's kind of place, and for a while he operated out of the Bradshaw family farm, by tradition a veritable den of thieves. He hit a bank in Stuttgart, Arkansas, one in Baxter Springs, Kansas, and probably another in Tryon, Oklahoma. Then it was a bank in Okmulgee with Bradshaw and Clarence Eno, one of still another set of poisonous brothers. Wilber, Bradshaw, and a third man topped the whole thing off by "hoorahing" the town of Vian, driving up and down the street, shooting up buildings and shouting at citizens.

Then the law began to have some luck. Two of the murderous Eno brothers were swept into the bag without resistance, in spite of being surrounded by a small arsenal. That seemed like the handwriting on the wall to Wilber, who moved farther west to a farm near Konawa, a sometimes hideout run by a man named Nash.

Nash was father-in-law to Champ Patterson, who was arrested in Boley, Oklahoma, after a failed bank robbery. He wasn't hard to catch, for he was horizontal, full of shotgun shot. His partners in crime, a driver named Glass and Pretty Boy Floyd's right arm, George Birdwell, ended up permanently dead. It was a bank raid gone very bad, but apparently Wilber learned no lessons from it.

Wilber started on his road to grief in Coalgate, Oklahoma, county seat of Coal County. How the law found out he was there is not clear, but officers staked out a residence of which they may have learned from a wedding license brazenly obtained under the name "Underhill" (yes, Wilber was out for another round of matrimonial sport).

Meanwhile, Wilber and three other hoodlums hit a bank in Frankfort, Kentucky. And they weren't getting all the headlines, which may have been an irritation to Wilber. A lot of the criminal activity just then involved three hoodlums whose method was to break into a business, pull a wire cable inside, attach it to the store safe, and then winch it onto their truck. The robbers—who included Ma Barker's vile child Herman—did well for a while, spreading their operation over a three-state area until the law caught up with them.

The system looked like a winner to Wilber, so he tried it in Harrah, Oklahoma. But he and his cohorts tried to steal too large a bank safe from too fragile a building, and succeeded only in dragging the safe until it broke through the floor and dropped into the basement.

Nothing daunted, Wilber returned to robbery the good old-fashioned way, hitting a bank in Coalgate with some helpers. They got some money, all right, but the law got an excellent description of their car, the same one they'd used in Harrah. That's when Wilber's luck ran completely out, for the local officers launched a search, got lucky, and spotted the car in front of the Nash house. They summoned up lots of help, but while they were questioning Nash,

Wilber heard them and fled out another entrance. He was wearing only his long johns, but he was carrying part of the Coalgate loot and a pair of Luger automatics.

Wilber made it to his car and roared away. The officers tried to follow, but lost him when their car got stuck. That did not stop the law. They had an address in the city of Shawnee where Wilber was supposed to be, and the police–federal agent task force descended on the Shawnee house. It was good information; Wilber's car was indeed there. The officers could see a light at the back of the building and heard sounds as of revelry in progress inside.

They did a little window peeping, and, sure enough, there was Wilber, again in only his long johns. His wife was with him, and it turned out that in the next room was another career hoodlum named Ralph Roe, and he too had a woman with him. The lead officer summoned Wilber to surrender; the outlaw answered "OK" and promptly produced another Luger with a high-capacity snail drum attached.

The officers didn't challenge a second time, but cut loose with shotguns and Thompsons. As his wife fainted, Wilber ran, pausing for a split second to return the officers' fire. He sprinted out the front door, only to run into more officers, who promptly opened fire. Wilber fell and lay still for a moment, then jumped to his feet and ran away between two neighboring houses. The officers pursued.

The second crook surrendered, hit a couple of times by rounds that punched through the wall between his bedroom and Wilber's. Sadly, the woman with him had been hit, too. But Wilber was still on his feet and still on the run. He didn't get far, just sixteen blocks, although it is a wonder he made it that far. For he was desperately wounded, and at last sought refuge in a furniture store, then closed for the night.

The lawmen were right behind him, and for once Wilber wasn't doing any fighting. He was lying on a bed, which was soaked with his blood; his Luger was close to him, but he did not reach for it. "I'm shot to hell," he said. "They got me five times." In fact,

Wilber had taken four .45 steel-jacketed bullets, plus several pieces of buckshot. He was hauled off to the Shawnee hospital forthwith, but nobody held out much hope for his recovery.

Back at the house where the evening's festivities had begun, officers found the usual arsenal: another Luger—this one with a folding stock—three other pistols, two sawed-off shotguns, and a rifle.

At the hospital, examination of what was left of Wilber's battered body revealed that he was indeed "shot to hell." The worst wound was a round into the back, which had torn into one kidney and his bladder. The other wounds were probably fixable, but that one was not. Wilber lasted several days until, to improve security, he was finally moved down to the hospital ward at McAlester prison.

And there, on the night of January 6, 1934, Wilber shuffled off to his reward, whatever that would turn out to be. And as usual, mother Almira had something weird to say about the whole affair. For openers, she said her son couldn't possibly have done everything he was accused of—she said things like that a lot—and finished with a reprise of a slightly earlier apologia that included this deathless line: "There has never been a disgrace in our family before."

She must have had a short memory.

Chapter 16

EVIL

Lawrence DeVol

MANY ROBBERS, MAYBE MOST, were simple sociopaths, but Lawrence DeVol was something infinitely worse. He was probably psychotic, at least somebody who would fascinate any psychiatrist, surely a human organism without any human feeling at all. He only lasted a little more than thirty-one destructive years before he departed this earth, but in that time this hollow sadist left a trail of death unrivaled in the history of American crime. If anybody was worse scum than Underhill, it was surely DeVol.

In addition to robberies, burglaries, and safe-crackings almost innumerable, he is known to have been responsible for the deaths of eleven people, six of whom were lawmen. There may have been more corpses littered along his back trail, for he was suspected in other killings, including contract assassinations. The eleven are only the ones we are sure of; there are probably more, maybe a lot more.

He was Ohio-born back in 1903 and moved with his family to Oklahoma while he was still a child. He apparently grew up fast, so fast that at the tender age of eleven he was consigned as "incorrigible" to something called the Oklahoma State Training School for White Boys.

Murder was his hobby: Larry DeVol.

MINNESOTA HISTORICAL SOCIETY

He spent only a short time at the school—which probably was little more for him than a graduate school in petty crime. In any case, he emerged to become a member of the collection of punks called the Central Park Gang, in Tulsa. Among the other hoodlums who were gang members were no less than three of the noxious Barker brothers, Freddie, Lloyd, and Arthur.

Arrested again for larceny at thirteen, he weathered that rap and went on studying crime with the gang until he joined three journeymen holdup men in robbing a bank in Vinton, Iowa. One of his colleagues was Harvey Bailey, certainly the shrewdest and best planner in the robbery ranks.

Larry was learning from the best, but he studiously ignored one of Bailey's governing rules. Bailey avoided violence whenever possible; he was ready to shoot if he had to, but he was not a killer. Larry DeVol sought out violence and genuinely liked killing.

That first robbery produced seventy thousand dollars, a very great deal of money in the summer of 1927, but it only whetted DeVol's appetite. And so, in the following February, he happily joined in a quarter-million-dollar bank robbery in an Ohio town called Washington Court House.

His career was interrupted temporarily by a conviction for a 1928 robbery gone wrong. He ended up in the Kansas prison at Hutchinson, and there he met his future friend and mentor, Alvin Karpis, sometimes called—for good reason—Creepy Karpis. The pair couldn't wait to resume their life of crime, and so they escaped from prison in March of 1929. Their flight took them through Pueblo, Colorado, where they stole a car and headed for Woodward, Oklahoma.

The pair tried to break into a store in Woodward but managed to bungle that simple operation—vicious the two surely were, but also not very bright. Karpis was arrested and sent back to prison, but DeVol got away.

In less than three months, he hit a bank with Bailey and four other pros, including journeyman outlaws Frank "Jelly" Nash and Francis Keating. That robbery, in Ottumwa, Iowa, fattened their wallets by some forty thousand dollars. The gang hit an even bigger jackpot in September 1930 with a raid on a bank in Lincoln, Nebraska. That was a fine payday, something in the neighborhood of two and a half million dollars, although most of that was in bonds.

DeVol's piece of the loot apparently didn't last long—or he was simply addicted to hurting people—for in November he staged a lone-hand raid on, of all things, a theater in Hannibal, Missouri. Along the way, however, Officer George Scrivens approached DeVol's car and asked him to step out of it.

The response was a hail of .45 slugs, one of which struck Scrivens and knocked him down. DeVol then turned on Scrivens' partner, Night Marshal John Rose, who was hit twice and went down on the street dying. Scrivens got to his feet, but was hit again high up on one leg. He emptied his pistol at the robber, sadly without hitting anything.

DeVol was long gone, but his fingerprints stayed behind, and from now on he was high on every lawman's list.

He now appeared as a sort of hired gun, a rumrunner on the side, and a killer for hire, paid by the piece. Mostly he worked as an enforcer, and he is known to have also participated in the beating of a speakeasy owner and the attempted murder of an uncooperative sheriff.

He killed a bootlegger who defied the local booze monopoly and a second man who also ran an illicit moonshine still. By then the police were turning over every rock searching for him, so DeVol wisely decided another climate would be better for him.

And so he next appears in St. Paul, Minnesota—he really got around—and there he joined the Barker gang, led by Freddie—called Shorty—another one of Ma Barker's poisonous sons. It was a sort of for-old-times'-sake reunion, for Alvin Karpis was part of the bunch as well, and DeVol had run with Fred Barker in the gang days in Tulsa. Other big outlaw names joined the gang from time to time, including Bailey, Keating, and Jelly Nash.

And for a time it seemed that this band of punks had found the golden road to riches. They got a quarter of a million dollars from a

Minneapolis bank in March of 1932, and forty-seven thousand more a couple of months later down in Fort Scott, Kansas. They struck another $250,000 bonanza in Concordia, Kansas, in July, although part of the loot was in bonds, not always easy to turn into cash.

The next job, up in a small town in North Dakota, was a comparative flop—only sixty-nine hundred dollars. His comrades on that job included Karpis, Freddie Barker, and another dull tool of a Barker kid, christened Arthur, but known in the criminal trade as Doc or Dock (he also, somewhat unoriginally, sometimes called himself Bob Barker, as a sort of unconvincing alias).

This raid was notable for a ferocious reaction by citizens and lawmen, driving the outlaws out of town in a hail of gunfire. Two women hostages were wounded in the chase, which ended, as usual, at the state line. The gang stole a Minnesota man's automobile and disappeared. The women were left lying in the grass behind a farm building; the police found and rescued them, but it was pure happenstance that they were found at all.

The police found that the car the thugs left behind was specially modified for outlaw work, with armor in the trunk to deflect bullets from pursuers and a specially altered backseat that faced to the rear, presumably to accommodate gang members firing on the pursuit.

Before the year was out, DeVol was part of a Minneapolis holdup that got twenty-two thousand dollars in real money and almost one hundred thousand in bonds.

Aside from the amount of loot, this job went very wrong indeed: Outside the bank DeVol killed police officers Leo Gorski and Ira Evans. The two officers had been called by a citizen who believed—correctly—that a robbery might be in progress.

The two officers, working together, drove up to the bank, but before they could even get out of their patrol car, DeVol cut loose with a submachine gun at a range of only about fifteen feet. Other gang members fired on the officers from inside the bank, smashing out the bank windows in the process.

Neither officer had a chance. Evans started to get out the driver's door and draw his pistol, but he never made it, slumping half in, half out of the car with his head on the running board. He had been hit ten times. Gorski managed to get out of the car, but he didn't manage to get off a shot either. Hit in the chest, stomach, and leg, he fell to the pavement. He was still alive, and civilian good Samaritans put him in their car and rushed to the hospital. He arrived still alive and even conscious, but he'd been torn up too badly by outlaw bullets.

That was bad enough, but while the gang was following their standard procedure, moving weaponry and loot to their "switch" getaway car, Fred Barker killed Oscar Erickson. He was an unsuspecting citizen who saw the switch in progress and slowed down, thinking the men around the two cars might need help.

He got no thanks, just a bullet in the head. He made it to the hospital, but the doctors could not save him. Since DeVol was part of the same gang, that made him a principal to this murder as well.

The law caught up with Larry DeVol after this one. He was arrested in St. Paul because of his vile temper, after he was found drunk and waving a gun in an apartment building. Two officers arrested him, but only after a violent struggle for the gun. DeVol bit one of the officers during the struggle and was subdued only after one of the officers bashed him in the head with his revolver. Only after the officers won the battle did they find out whom they had arrested.

So DeVol celebrated Christmas of 1932 with second-degree murder convictions for the killings of Officers Evans and Gorski and a life sentence. He had pleaded guilty to murder, of all things, but it was not a mistake and it certainly was not out of remorse, an emotion entirely alien to him. He did it to avoid being shipped to Missouri to answer charges for killing another policeman in Kirksville. It was a simple decision: Minnesota had no death penalty; Missouri did.

Off he went to the state prison at Stillwater, Minnesota, long-time home to the Younger brothers after their disastrous try in 1876 at robbing the little bank in Northfield. He immediately became a prodigious pain in the behind, mouthing off to the guard staff and threatening that he had friends who would "take care of him" and since he had murdered "one or two" a few more wouldn't matter. DeVol spent much of 1934 in and out of solitary confinement. He missed the big show on the outside, although he must have heard about it: That was the year the law ran down Pretty Boy Floyd, Bonnie and Clyde, John Dillinger, Baby Face Nelson, and Wilber Underhill, as vile a specimen as DeVol. None of those stars of the world of crime survived their meetings with the law, which was hardly surprising, given those outlaws' penchant for killing people. In every case the famous names of crime ended up quite dead.

But DeVol didn't stay in Stillwater prison as he was intended to. Besides threatening the guard staff with murder, he declared darkly that he was innocent, the warden was out to kill him, his food was poisoned, and on and on.

Either because he put on a convincing act or because he really wasn't running on all eight cylinders, he was transferred to St. Peter's Hospital for the Criminally Insane. He could not have wished for more. Inevitably, DeVol broke out in 1936, along with some fifteen other more-or-less crazy criminal inmates. He promptly returned to what he did best.

Retribution had been a long time coming to Larry DeVol, but it caught up with him after he and another punk robbed a bank in Turon, Kansas. He made a run for Oklahoma, and there the end of the road came in the city of Enid. The police surrounded him there, in a dive called the German Village Tavern; right in character, DeVol chose to start shooting. Tragically, Officer Cal Palmer died and another lawman was wounded before the remaining officers filled DeVol full of holes—lots of them. To everybody's relief, he remained permanently dead.

There was no noticeable mourning for DeVol's passing. His epitaph, had there been one, would have been simple: "*Good riddance.*"

Chapter 17

IF IT WEREN'T FOR BAD LUCK, WE'D HAVE NO LUCK AT ALL

The Bank of Gore and Kaiser Bill

THE DEPRESSION HADN'T HIT just yet; that misery was still in the future, but things were not easy for farmers throughout Oklahoma, and that was bad enough for this struggling little farming community called Gore, Oklahoma. Still, the local bank managed to stay solvent—it was the Farmers State Bank of Illinois—and most businesses were at least able to get by. The people of Gore and the country 'round about were tough and resilient; they were willing to hang on and build for the future until better days came around.

What they didn't need was the attention of the trash of the countryside, the worthless sloths who were willing to rob and kill other people in preference to working for a living. There were lots of them, too, particularly in the Cookson Hills, an easy jaunt away, and in the Osage country.

Much has been written about the "gangs" of the Cookson Hills, but that term is a little misleading. In fact, though there were indeed loosely organized bands of outlaws, the personnel often changed according to who wanted to go on the next job, who was wanted by the law and opted to stay in hiding, who was in jail, and who'd been blown away by the law. Still, the Cooksons were a hive of bad men, and Gore was handy for them. You could go to Gore, steal a wad of money, and be back in the hills in plenty of time for dinner.

The first unwelcome visit to Gore was back in 1918, when three robbers on horseback hit the bank, an unholy trio of professional trash. Mount Cookson was the scion of a prominent family—in fact, the hills had been named for one of his ancestors—but Mount was turning out to be the family disgrace. He managed ultimately to die from natural causes, but only after a dreary lifetime spent in and out of prison in Oklahoma and Arkansas. Among other foibles, he was brother-in-law to professional crook Kie Carlile.

With him rode one Fred Walker, like Mount a professional criminal by choice. Walker was nicknamed Cotton and was a career badman. His specialty was more planning and manipulating than actively leading raids and pistol waving, but this time he rode along with Mount and a third man.

The third man was a strange character who'd spent a lifetime—quite literally—breaking the law. His real name seems to have been Bill Goodman, although he had a flock of aliases, but he had caught the interest of the press; so he was also called the Fagin of the Cooksons and the Old Man of the Hills. And, most famously, he was best known as Kaiser Bill for an astonishing spread of droopy mustache that made him look a little like Wilhelm, the German emperor so well known during World War I.

Kaiser Bill had a long string of robberies to his credit—if that's the word—and had otherwise spent much of his long life in the slammer. He'd done several hitches in various prisons—including two in Leavenworth—and maybe others elsewhere under one or more of his divers aliases. He was a very senior citizen, but that didn't stop him. He and his fellow thugs rode off with a little over three thousand dollars, a tidy sum for the day.

This might be the place to say that there wasn't any friendly FDIC until 1933, so a looted bank had to absorb all the loss unless it had private insurance against robbery. If it went under, its depositors, ordinary people like the farmer and the small businessman, lost

If it weren't for bad luck, we'd have no luck at all.
The bank of Gore and Kaiser Bill.

their savings. So much for the myth of the gallant western Robin Hood, which is unadulterated poppycock except in Hollywood. Men like Cookson and Kaiser Bill cheerfully stole from rich and poor alike, without any petty partiality. If they preferred to rob the rich, it was only because the rich had more money.

The next trouble for little Gore popped up in 1920, in the form of still another visit by robbers, in this case one Bush—short for Bushyhead—Wood and, who else, Kaiser Bill, back for a second helping. He must have liked the little town of Gore, or at least its bank. Cookson and Walker may have been along on this one, too, but nobody today is entirely sure. This time the bandits got a couple of grand, still a good day's pay for just a few minutes of waving guns around and talking tough.

All of this was bad enough for the little town and its bank, but there was worse to come. In the autumn of 1921, the long-suffering bank was burgled, and then, just three months later, it was visited again by horseback bandits.

This time it was another veteran professional robber, Ed Lockhart, and a second man, probably an Arkansas punk named Brodie. Lockhart was a pro, suspected in at least eight bank robberies and probably involved in more than that.

He and the other man got around sixteen hundred dollars. It wasn't quite as much as the hauls reaped in the earlier robberies, but for the bank's operators it was, as the western saying went, all she wrote. The bank closed its doors and left Gore without a financial institution, often the kiss of death for a small rural town.

Just a few hours before the heist from the Gore bank, robbers had hit the Bank of Northern Arkansas at a wide spot in the road called Everton. Since even Ed Lockhart couldn't have been in two places at very nearly the same time, the bandit was obviously somebody else. In all probability the other Lockhart was brother Sam, emulating his sibling in the pursuit of other people's money.

The law was on the alert and so were ordinary citizens. This time it panned out. A Tahlequah haberdasher became suspicious of a man who fitted himself out with new clothes, a gold watch, and a derby hat and paid cash for his new purchases from a monstrous wad of currency.

The sheriff was very interested when the clothier told him about the exhibition of all that money, and picked up the buyer, who was carrying not only his roll—in the neighborhood of thirteen hundred dollars—but also pockets full of gold coins. The gold totaled precisely the amount of gold coin stolen from the Arkansas bank.

This dummy turned out to be one L.W. Sitton, who, it developed, was related by marriage to none other than Ed Lockhart. Nothing like keeping it in the family. Sitton wouldn't talk much past giving his name, and he certainly wouldn't name his companions in the Arkansas robbery. His reticence was all very noble, but it cost him ten years in the Arkansas pen.

The law didn't give up on Lockhart. A reward was offered for him—and, incidentally, for his brother Sam, following along in the family tradition. Ed was well-known to law enforcement: He'd run for years with Henry Starr, the whiny, self-invented King of the Bank Robbers. Lockhart had certainly been with Starr on several raids and was identified or a suspect in at least eight or ten more.

Lockhart got his comeuppance at the hands of lawman Mont Grady after a hand-to-hand struggle during an attempt to arrest Lockhart. Going up to a home at which Lockhart was eating breakfast, Grady found himself looking into the ugly end of Lockhart's rifle. The outlaw took Grady's revolver and shoved it in his own pocket. Grady's predicament made other officers back off, but one of them fired a round that distracted Lockhart long enough for Grady to knock the rifle muzzle to one side.

The lawman struggled with Lockhart and in the process managed to shove his hand into the robber's pocket where his own pistol was stashed. He got his finger on the trigger and pulled it, and the round caught Lockhart in the abdomen. He fell and managed to say the obvious: "My God, you've killed me." Sure enough, he had that right. At least Lockhart had finished his long criminal career without killing anybody, although there was no doubt he was ready to.

And he had a brilliant war record, which made his criminal behavior that much sadder. So veterans organizations helped out with his funeral, and a great many people attended the viewing and the burial. It was a far cry from the end of Kaiser Bill.

For even Kaiser Bill at last found his own dead end, after a lifetime spent in prison or terrorizing people he didn't even know. When he took on the bank in Ketchum, Oklahoma, it wasn't the first time for this bank. They'd been robbed before, back in 1923, and their cashier had been murdered in the process.

This time the bank men were looking at an old man brandishing a long-barreled revolver and a younger man with an automatic, who turned out to be a nonentity named Bill Quinton. Quinton had no record that anybody ever found, but he was going to school with the old master. There was no shooting, but the bandits took a hostage with them when they fled, the current cashier, a young man named Gregory, son of the bank president.

Released the better part of a mile away, young Gregory ran back to the bank and collected his father and another man. The three gave chase, as did a multitude of citizens and lawmen from the whole area.

Fittingly, it was the bank men who came up with the outlaws, who unaccountably were parked when they should have been making tracks far away from the bank. They were standing talking on the shoulder of the road with a third man. The bankers assumed the extra man was the getaway driver, but in fact he was unconnected with the robbery. The robbers had changed the license plates on their car, but had not promptly resumed their retreat, just another in the long, long history of moronic bandit mistakes.

The bandits opened fire on the bank men's car, mortally wounding the elder Gregory. Kaiser Bill's gun malfunctioned after just a couple of rounds, but young Gregory's automatic did not. He got two slugs into the gray head of Kaiser Bill, whereof the patriarch of Cookson criminals forthwith expired. The third bank man pulled down on Bill's young colleague with a rifle and extinguished him as well. Sadly, in the exchange the third man, the innocent, also died.

So passed Kaiser Bill Goodman—or whatever his real name was—alumnus of various prisons, robber of nobody knew how many rural banks and country stores. He ended up as ingloriously as he had lived, planted in potter's field at Vinita. There seem to have been no mourners.

Nobody gave a damn.

AFTERWORD

HE BROUGHT IT ON HISSELF

ROBBERS OF ALL KINDS are still very much with us, professional and otherwise. They range from the punks who rob elderly people on the street for their social security checks to the career outlaws who rob banks and armored cars. There is no redeeming social value to any of them, in spite of considerable romanticizing by book and article writers who ought to know better.

There is a tendency to excuse such people for a variety of unconvincing reasons. They come from a dysfunctional family, or they lived in a slum, or they're not very bright, or they were bullied as children—whatever the explanation for their lawless behavior, it was somebody else's fault.

Perhaps part of the explanation for their vile behavior is simpler than that. Some people are simply scum by nature, unwilling to live by anybody else's rules, or too lazy to work for a living, or both. Or maybe it just gives them pleasure to hurt people. Those people are sadists, or psychotic, or both. They and their apologists can find an infinite number of excuses for them, but Shakespeare saw human nature more clearly. He put it succinctly in *Julius Caesar*:

> The fault, dear Brutus, is not in our stars,
> but in ourselves, that we are underlings.

Or, as my lawman grandfather more plainly said of the train robber he killed near Deadwood, "He brought it on hisself."

Granddad, Texas John Slaughter, and Grover Bishop had it right: The only good outlaw is a dead outlaw.

BIBLIOGRAPHY

Block, Eugene B., *Great Train Robberies* (London: Alvin Redman, 1964).

Burton, Arthur T., *Black, Red and Deadly* (Austin: Eakin Press, 1991).

Butler, Ken, *More Oklahoma Renegades* (Gretna, LA: Pelican Press, 2007).

Cain, Del, *Lawmen of the Old West: The Bad Guys* (Plano, TX: Republic of Texas Press, 2001).

Chrisman, Harry E., *Fifty Years on the Owl Hoot Trail* (Chicago: Sage Books, 1969).

Chrisman, Harry E., *Lost Trails of the Cimarron* (Norman, OK: University of Oklahoma Press, 1998).

Cunningham, Eugene, *Triggernometry: A Gallery of Gunfighters* (Caldwell, ID: Caxton Printers, 1989).

Dalton, Emmett, *Beyond the Law* (Coffeyville, KS: Coffeyville Historical Society, n.d.).

DeArment, Robert, *Bravo of the Brazos* (Norman, OK: University of Oklahoma Press, 2002).

DeArment, Robert, *Forgotten Gunfighters of the Old West,* vol. 2 (Norman, OK: University of Oklahoma Press, 2007).

DeArment, Robert, *Knights of the Green Cloth* (Norman, OK: University of Oklahoma Press, 1982).

DeArment, Robert, *Twelve Forgotten Gunfighters of the Old West* (Norman, OK: University of Oklahoma Press, 2003).

Edge, L.L., *Run the Cat Roads* (New York: Dembner Books, 1981).

Elman, Robert, *Badmen of the West* (Secaucus, NJ: Ridge Press, 1974).

Erdoes, Richard, *Saloons of the Old West* (New York: Gramercy Press, 1979).

Ernst, Robert R., *Robbin' Banks and Killin' Cops* (Baltimore: Publish America, 2009).

Farris, David A., *Oklahoma Outlaw Tales* (Edmond, OK: Little Bruce, 2004).

Fisher, O.C., and Jeff C. Dykes, *King Fisher: His Life and Times* (Norman, OK: University of Oklahoma Press, 1966).

Fradkin, Philip L., *Stagecoach* (New York: Simon & Schuster Source, 2002).

Freeman, G.D., *Midnight and Noonday* (Norman, OK: University of Oklahoma Press, 1984).

Fulton, Maurice G., *History of the Lincoln County War* (Tucson, AZ: University of Arizona Press, 2008).

Garrett, Pat F., *The Authentic Life of Billy the Kid* (New York: Indian Head Books, 1994).

Gibson, A.M., *The Life and Death of Colonel Albert Jennings Fountain* (Norman, OK: University of Oklahoma Press, 1965).

Helmer, William J., and Rick Mattix, *The Complete Public Enemy Almanac* (Nashville, TN: Cumberland House, 2007).

Horan, James D., *Desperate Women* (New York: Bonanza Books, 1952).

Koch, Michael, *The Kimes Gang* (Bloomington, IN: AuthorHouse, 2005).

McCarty, John L., *Maverick Town* (Norman, OK: University of Oklahoma Press, 1988).

McPherson, M.A., and Eli McLaren, *Outlaws and Lawmen of the Old West*, vol. 1 (Renton, WA: Lone Pine Publishing, 2000).

Metz, Leon Claire, *Pat Garrett* (Norman, OK: University of Oklahoma Press, 1974).

Metz, Leon Claire, *The Shooters* (El Paso, TX: Mangan Books, 1976).

Miller, Nyle H., and Joseph W. Snell, *Great Gunfighters of the Kansas Cowtowns* (Lincoln, NE: University of Nebraska Press, 1963).

Morgan, R.D., *Bad Boys of the Cookson Hills* (Stillwater, OK: New Forums Press, 2002).

Morgan, R.D., *Bandit Kings of the Cookson Hills* (Stillwater, OK: New Forums Press, 2003).

Morgan, R.D., *The Tri-State Terror* (Stillwater, OK: New Forums Press, 2005).

Nash, Jay Robert, *Encyclopedia of Western Lawmen and Outlaws* (New York: Da Capo Press, 1994).

Nolan, Frederick, *The Lincoln County War* (Norman, OK: University of Oklahoma Press, 1992).

O'Neal, Bill, *Encyclopedia of Western Gunfighters* (Norman, OK: University of Oklahoma Press, 1979).

O'Neal, Bill, *Henry Brown: The Outlaw-Marshal* (College Station, TX: Creative Publishing Co., 1980).

Parsons, Chuck, and Marianne E. Hall Little, *Captain L.H. McNelly* (Austin, TX: State House Press, 2001).

Rasch, Phillip K., *Warriors of Lincoln County* (Stillwater, OK: NOLA, 1998).

Shirley, Glenn, *Marauders of the Indian Nations* (Stillwater, OK: Barbed Wire Press, 1994).

Shirley, Glenn, *Thirteen Days of Terror* (Stillwater, OK: Barbed Wire Press, 1996).

Smith, Robert Barr, *Daltons!* (Norman, OK: University of Oklahoma Press, 1996).

Smith, Robert Barr, *Last Hurrah of the James Younger Gang* (Norman, OK: University of Oklahoma Press, 2001).

Smith, Robert Barr, *Outlaw Tales of Oklahoma* (Guilford, CT: Globe Pequot Press, 2008).

Smith, Robert Barr, "A Second Career: The Odyssey of Elmer McCurdy." *Wild West*, June 1999.

Smith, Robert Barr, *Tough Towns* (Guilford, CT: Globe Pequot Press, 2007).

Vaughn, Columbus, and Frank Snow, *This Was Frank Dalton* (Philadelphia: Dorrance and Co., 1969).

West, C.W. (Dub), *Outlaws and Peace Officers of Indian Territory* (Muskogee, OK: Muskogee Publishing Co., 1987).

Wilson, H. Michael, *Great Stagecoach Robberies* (Guilford, CT: Globe Pequot Press, 2007).

Yadon, Lawrence J., and Robert Barr Smith, *Old West Swindlers* (Gretna, LA: Pelican Press, 2011).

ARTICLES AND INTERVIEWS

Afton *Weekly Herald*, 2 November 1894.

All figures from Fradkin, *Stagecoach*, 95*ff.*

Beaver *Herald*, 4 April 1895.

Cherokee Advocate, 6 February 1895.

Cheyenne *Sunbeam*, 5 April 1895.

Daily Oklahoman, 28 October 1894.

Edmond *Sun-Democrat*, 5 April 1895.

Eufaula, I.T. *Indian Journal*, 5 April 1895.

"Hiram Stevens." www.okolha.net/hiramstevens.htm

Indian Journal, 5 April 1895.

Indian Journal, 15 February 1895.

Indian Journal, 11 November 1894.

Indian-Pioneer Papers: Albert King Barry interview.

Indian-Pioneer Papers: G.W. Slater interview.

Indian-Pioneer Papers: James W. Turley interview.

Indian-Pioneer Papers: Roy Toombs statement.

Indian-Pioneer Papers: S.W. Ross interview.

Indian Pioneer Papers: William Byrd interview.

Indian-Pioneer Papers: Winifred M. Clark interview.

Muskogee *Indian Journal*, 22 June 1894.

Muskogee *Phoenix*, 23 April 1896.

Muskogee *Phoenix*, 19 March 1896.

Weekly Elevator, 5 April 1895.

INDEX

INDEX

ABOUT THE AUTHOR

ROBERT BARR SMITH is a law professor at the University of Oklahoma and a retired colonel, U.S. Army. He is the author of seven books and nearly one hundred articles on western and military history. A senior parachutist, he served in Vietnam, Germany, and all across the United States. He is a frequent lecturer on the West.